A LIGHT ROAST:
Conversations with My Dead Dad

eBook ISBN: 979-8-9985198-8-8
Paperback ISBN: 979-8-9934026-1-1
Hardcover ISBN: 979-8-9934026-3-5

Cover design by K. Nickerson

Edited by Hilary Jastram, www.bookmarkpub.com

A Light Roast

Conversations with my Dead Dad

A SUPERNATURAL MEMOIR BY

Jen (and Bud) Stefanski

For Mama Jean

Get In Touch

Jenstefanskiauthor.com

Contents

*"Always go to other people's funerals.
Otherwise, they won't come to yours."*

—Yogi Berra

Foreword

A few months ago, my mom and I called my sister. We like to talk on the phone, the three of us. It saves time repeating what was said, which we always end up doing anyway. Jenny said she was glad to have us both on the line. She had something big to share and instantly burst into tears. (Very typical of Jenny. She has the Italian curse of crying over any big piece of news, embarrassment, or empathetic tertiary pain felt by people she's never met. The primary reason she is a lawyer who stays out of the courtroom.) Back to the crying …

I thought someone had died. My mom thought Jenny was pregnant (definitely worse than death to Jenny). No. She had written a book. Okay … and it's about Dad. Okay … it's about conversations with Dad … But he's already dead … and he's giving advice *from beyond* the grave that he doesn't even have.

The middle child in me wanted to react in an affirming way to my baby sister: "Wow, that is awesome, Jenny. Good for you! You are an author." **Inside**: *What in the actual hell is happening right now?* **Outside**: "Oh yes, I will read it, and oh yes, so wonderful." **Inside**: *I have to relive the loss … I have to look through the lens of my sister's imagination and revisit his opinions.* Only natural as one of his kids to apply them to all of the decisions I've made for the past seven years. Wrap your brain around that.

It took me six months to read this book. Sixty-some printer pages of fatherly advice. I couldn't come back to it or even read it for more than 10-minute clips. I read it out of order, and my husband teased that I treated it like a *Choose Your Own Adventure book*: "For Dad's reaction to your parenting, turn to page 49."

In my defense, it's like this: The closer you are to someone who dies, the more guilt you have. The end. No, seriously, the closer you are to the dead, the more reason you have to analyze a conversation or replay an interaction, because that's the only way the human brain can truly manipulate you into thinking the death was your fault. *Why didn't you call him that extra time? Why did you say no to a dinner just because he was being difficult the night before? You could have saved him.*

Love is complex, as the world already knows, but parent and child love, now that is the matrix. And nobody gets to adulthood without some type of guilt or anger or regret, all wrapped up in this thick misconnection of family. But I read it. I finished the whole damn thing. Sober, thank you.

This book offers you some pretty sound transcendental advice. My sister was always Dad's favorite. As a mom of many, I can tell you from a sincere place that I have no animosity or jealousy whatsoever. They understand each other because *they see each other*. It's like a piece of his brain split off and grew into her brain. She's his starfish.

Grief is crazy because when he died, it wasn't just him I lost. Not just his crazy, brilliant, blunt advice. Not just his loud burps from the other room or genuine care wrapped in sarcasm, so it didn't get too heavy. I lost his relationship with my sister. I lost their banter and the joy they shared in each other's presence. I lost a piece of my sister that would never come back. Until this book. This strange odyssey that I have come to realize was co-authored by my dad and his starfish.

–Robyn Stefanski Marsh
Immediate Family Member of the Authors

Well ... how did I get here?

Originally, I started this book to hang out with my dad. I'd play his classic rock and listen as his voice would come in over the beat to tell me "what's what." It was a selfish and comforting project and one I thought (hoped?) my family might enjoy one day. I chose writing instead of grief therapy, and I think my writing group was onto me there. I also wanted to see if I could bring Bud back into the physical world in any shape or form, even if that shape were a paperback, something I could hold in my hands (maybe read on the toilet?).

> But as I shared these conversations, I learned how universal grief is, and just how many of us are crying in cars and talking on toilets.

In these talks we have, Bud is no angel—he is a whole person, and that's what makes him human again. Bud represents the realities of functional addicts. Addiction in movies is always so dramatic and shattering, as it often can be. But sometimes it's subtle, creating slight cracks in the foundation that a family has to dance around. And it doesn't define the person. They may be hard to live with, but you don't want to live without them.

So, that's why I wrote this. And I will miss my writing sessions with Bud, who changed the radio station too much in anticipation of the next song.

"I wish I was a messenger and all the news was good."

—Pearl Jam

I stood alone at a high-top table, eating shrimp at my aunt's funeral. Well, not at the *funeral,* if that's the church part. I mean the afterlife afterparty afterward part. There aren't formal funeral invitations. I'm perpetually confused about how I end up at a wake.

Somehow it starts at a church, a synagogue, a funeral parlor, where those closest to the deceased are forced to "welcome" you in a procession line, where you say, "I'm so sorry for your loss (*did you kill her?*)." and "Your mother was the best (*now who's the best?*)." Eventually, someone with authority announces, "The family that is grieving and on copious amounts of Valium or Ativan and/or Klonopin in order to listen to your boilerplate condolences on repeat all morning would now like to buy you lunch."

So, there I was, eating the greatest shrimp of my life at a country club I couldn't remember being invited to. I'm certain that's the only thing I managed to say that day to my uncle, husband of the deceased, brother, and pre-mortem best friend to my dead dad. "This is the greatest shrimp I've ever eaten." He agreed. I'm good at condolences.

My aunt's funeral was the first one I'd been to since my dad's sudden death, 17 months and 7 days earlier. Its attendance was at least 50% of the same Irish Catholic cast of characters that would have been at his funeral, had we disregarded his agnostic wishes and had one.

I marveled at my cousins, greeting grievers for hours, giving a eulogy. But mostly I pitied them. I knew this wasn't the saddest part. That would come a little later and would be that agony that remains in some dull fashion "forever and ever, amen." I cried that day for my cousins' loss, but also for what I knew was coming for them: nothing.

I cried for my aunt, a Dancing Queen with an ornery streak and one of those perfect throaty chuckles. I cried for the narcissist in me who kept imagining it was my dad's funeral. I cried from a sick jealousy that my cousins got to say goodbye, "got to" watch their mother die from a decade of cancer. It's the age-old rivalry between griever types. The loved ones of those suffering long illnesses are jealous of those of us who lose our people quick, thinking it was less painful for the dead. Those of us who lose our people in an instant are jealous of those who get to say what we imagine is some movie-scripted goodbye. It's *Terms of Endearment*, isn't it? After a long illness, the piano and flutes begin to play, and there are knowing, loving looks exchanged with the dying. A nurse comes in and, with a peaceful whisper, announces, "He's gone," as the family embraces. I don't buy it. It's all the same hell, different type of torture.

> *My father's favorite oxymoron: devout agnostic.*
>
> *My favorite: jumbo shrimp.*

It tasted so good it didn't even need cocktail sauce, but I slathered it on anyway, as one of my father's many cousins approached my solo high-top as I bit into two jumbos at once. I don't know what side of the family he was, but I knew he was related: same round head, rosy cheeks, Irish eyes "a smilin,'" gold rimmed glasses, white rim of hair, suit and tie with neither quite as long as it needed to be.

"You're Bud's youngest, right?"

Am I still his kid if he's not here to claim me? I nodded, tugging shrimp tails through my clenched teeth.

"Yeah, I was talking to your Aunt Karen. She said you're funny, just like him."

He waited.

I stared.

Time stared back at both of us, waiting for a cue to move.

I wiped cocktail sauce from the corner of my mouth, cleaned my hands on the skirt of my standard funeral dress. *He wants you to make him laugh. At least say something clever. This is a family affair at a country club outside of Philadelphia. You know this crowd. He's either an alcoholic or a recovering alcoholic. But is he a Catholic or a recovering Catholic? Too many ways to play this, and yet none at all. Joke's on us because I'm not my dad.*

He had me cornered. I wanted to give him what he wanted, a good guttural chuckle right when it's needed most. Instead, he may as well have told me that they ran out of shrimp. *Where were my older siblings to break the silence?*

My brother knows everyone in our family tree, always has a knack for asking how the parents, the kids, the dogs, the former next-door neighbors are, and manages a fixed smile no matter the setting. My sister, a professional counselor, can ask complete strangers a cascade of insightful questions that have the potential to expose everything wrong with their marriage and why they blame their mother for their choices. I liked to watch it all go down with popcorn. I am the youngest, the baby who's rarely left alone, feeling exposed. Instructed to act "just like him," I could feel my shortness, his (and my, I guess?) signature trademark.

"This is the greatest shrimp I've ever eaten." My father's cousin exhaled, and his eyes darted over me in disappointment. He should try the shrimp.

For how small this encounter was, I think about it too often. But only because I'm waiting for the next punch. It's always repeated in some fashion. The latest was a lunch with my mom and my almost-atheist father's four former coworkers, all nuns. Driving home after, Mom said: "While you were in the bathroom, the nuns all said how much you're like him." The brain-racking began. *How? What did I do? What did I order? Did I blow my nose a lot? Did I belch? Shit, I know I didn't say fuck in front of nuns?* Their words are meant as a compliment—but it's a painful compliment. Like when someone consoles you with "You seem to be doing much better since the loss of your dad." They don't know how much I wish I *were* more like my dad, and the ways I'm glad I'm not.

I didn't repeat any of Dad's jokes. Most were dated or so vulgar that I was required to leave the room as a child. I have little of his full repertoire to go on. Those I remember are no longer socially acceptable, or they never were.

But I know things.

I know *him.*

I know that while he had some go-to raunchy jokes, it was his wit in the moment, his reading of a room that people really remember. He hated practical jokes, tricking your audience—the lowest form of comedy.

He had good funeral jokes, if that category exists. I can picture him at his grandmother's funeral. I didn't know my great-grandmother, but it sounds like she was a delicate pierogi from the Old Country. Not wanting to ever upset her, my dad said that when he was a kid, most conversations ended with "Don't tell Mom-Mom that happened." He claimed to have walked around her funeral, warning everyone: "Don't tell Mom-Mom she died." Whatever he would have said to his cousin that day would have gotten a beer-belly laugh.

I know that when my aunt Cathy died, he would have sat on the edge of his bed, cried a bit, and then pinched the bridge of his nose, ending with an *"Oh, shit"* sigh, cause when it comes to death, there ain't nothing you can do.

Once I realized my dad died (it took about six months to stop the instant wonder: *Why hasn't Dad called*?), I also realized that whenever I was alone, I would talk to him, and if I played my cards right, he'd answer back. My head knows it's *me* answering *me*. But some responses feel instantaneous, like I'm a defibrillator bringing him back, and others I can't seem to force. He either answers or he doesn't.

> *I've talked with him more than any daughter on a toilet should ever be talking to her father.*

Since he's died, he's only come to me once in a morbid, vivid dream. I put a hand on each of his cheeks like a game we played as kids, and he just let me stare into his face, and I mean *stare*. Time stood still for us, waiting. It was real at the time. And that was it. It's been years now, and nothing else. No birds, no butterflies, no pennies from heaven. He just talks. But he's not as mouthy as me.

People say that grief is the flipside of love and that the loved ones we lose are always in our hearts. Not this guy. He's in my head and won't shut the hell up. The tape deck of my mind plays scenes, clips, songs, one-liners. Sometimes, these tracks address what's happening in the present; sometimes, they get me the hell out of the present.

What I could have told that cousin looking for a funeral joke is: "Yes, we have the same eyes, small and set back. But his were vivid blue, while mine are watery and gray. Yes, we're both sarcastic, but his dry humor was clever and timed. Mine comes out harsh and polarizing. I don't know dirty jokes, and I don't drink scotch. I laugh at puns, and I like marijuana."

I would add: What he taught me is that most of what I want to say about life already exists in song lyrics, and is better than what I could say myself. As Dan Fogelberg knows, my life is a poor attempt to imitate that man.

The following are conversations I've had with my Leader of the Band since he died. Maybe they're not real, but they were real at the time. And if we don't listen to the voices in our head, then who are we going to listen to? For me, they're more interesting than any of the shit in the now.

> *"Send lawyers, guns, and money* Dad, *get me out of this."*
>
> —Warren Zevon

Right out of the (pearly) gates, you should know that I don't care how dead you are. You made this mess of regrets; now come clean it up. You were dubbed our *Chubb Rock*, the control freak who made us dependent on you, and then you went and died on us.

It's simple: it's all your fault, so come control this.

Sure, you had a bad heart that they found out about in your thirties. But you had choices, *years* of choices.

You were always lecturing your kids, teaching us how to have choices in life, yet you always made the wrong ones. You put off going to doctors, never exercised (bad heart = good excuse), ate Boar's Head pepperoni sticks, washed them down with Bud Light. You took care of us and not yourself.

> *While physically this is a real impossibility, it's extremely simple to me. Fucking fix all this pain because it's too heavy and I can't do it.*

I used to imagine you dying all the time, in that dramatic way you imagine something so tragic that it *doesn't* happen. I imagined you dying every time I watched you fail at the latest diet or start to exercise by taking a walk once in a row. Naively, I would only imagine how much it would hurt *me*. *My* loss, *my* grief.

I never imagined the pain of everyone else around me and how I wouldn't be able to make that stop, turn the volume down. So now you've failed your wife, your kids, your brothers, and your friends. Maybe don't fix it for me, but you sure as shit should fix it for them.

You loved sending Mom on trips. It became a hobby in your retirement. Since you hated the physical part of travel (you told me airport security once pulled you aside and "touched you in places Mom never had"), sending her on all those trips seemed like a way for you to see the world, too. But it's time to admit it was more than that. Send Mom away for a few weeks, and you could eat and drink (emphasis on *drink*) whatever you wanted.

You sent Mom to Luxembourg to stay with me for three weeks, and then during that time, you went away for good. That created an eternal case of the *What Ifs*.

What If I hadn't taken the temporary job in Luxembourg? Seems to me, if I'm not going to have kids (your advice), it's to give me the ability to travel or take temporary roles in exotic places like Luxembourg, which, it turns out, is really the Wilmington, Delaware of Europe.

What If, when my boss called me in June to come home early and take another role on the U.S. team, I'd done it?

What If Mom hadn't come to visit?

What If Mom hadn't come to visit *for so long*?

What If you had accepted the neighbor's invite to grill steaks? Would they have seen how sick you were getting? Or would they have chalked it up to your overall poor health? How could neighbors, even living across the street for 30 years, ever have convinced a stubborn curmudgeon like you to go to the hospital anyway?

Here are a few more:

What If you had taken care of yourself all those years?

What If you had listened to your doctors?

What If you had listened to your body that decade, that year, that month, that week, that day?

The *What Ifs* can go on forever. I refuse to play that game (she declares as she writes them all out).

And the most monumental *What If?*

What If it didn't all go down like this:

Mom lands in The Delaware of Europe. After one 25-minute double-decker open-air bus tour that tells you all you never needed to know about Luxembourg, we head off to Berlin to meet your firstborn, your son.

Bryan happened to be there for work, too. This is Friday, July 13th. We tour the Wall and marvel that it was still in operation in the not-so-distant '80s, not embarrassed enough by how little history we know.

> *Wait, Berlin was in* <u>*East*</u> *Germany? Hence the Wall. Ethnocentric American mind blown.*

Bryan heads home. I won't hear from him again until he calls to say you're gone. Mom and I take a train to Strasbourg, which, as the aforementioned ethnocentric Americans, we learn is in France. We walk along the Rhine and comment on how this Disney-set-of-a-town is exactly what we Americans expect *all* European towns to look like—even though we know the central square is not where currently-breathing-and-working people live. We eat Ethiopian food that night because, *When in Strasbourg*? This is Friday, July 20th. You have 72 hours left.

During Mom's stay, you pay international calling rates from your landline to talk every day. You did that for all her trips. You always let us report on the sights and ask questions: "What time is it there?" "How's the weather?" "What'd ya eat?" "Ethiopian food in France? Jesus Christ."

You always said our travels were "neat." You labeled things "neat," like my generation labels it "awesome." Is that left over from the '50s, along with dungarees? Neat.

> *On the 23rd, you never call. Later, Mom will say she knew then.*

On the 24th, Mom's lifelong girlfriends, Ginny and Mo, land in Luxembourg to stay with us. When the Besties' plane touches down from Long Island, the tiny town of Luxembourg experiences a rippling, cosmic shift as *so much* New York enters the Grand Duchy. Oh yes, I never got to tell you that Luxembourg is referred to as the Grand Duchy. Lots of missed pun opportunities there, Bud.

Boisterous Long Island (pronounced: Lawn GUY-lin) accented exclamations fill the marble lobby of my tiny apartment building as we attempt to help the Besties and their big-ass American luggage into the European shoebox-sized elevator, complete with its outer metal accordion door. These cage-like elevator doors remind me of those wooden retractable baby gates popular at our split-level house in the '80s. Remember those gates? Or should I say, do you remember when, as a crawling baby, I put my melon through one of the diamond openings, causing both sides of the gate to dislodge from the walls and the accordion to shut on my neck?

Bryan, all of eight, ran to get you as I turned blue. You pried opened the accordion as best you could, took your pudgy, doesn't-know-how-to-use-a-hammer hand and forced my noggin right the hell back through that gate. If that's parenthood, no thank you. I *lived*, and it still gives me an adrenaline rush. To this day, I hate turtlenecks and tight necklaces. The '90s choker necklace era was really tough for me. I replay that story in my head whenever Bryan and I disagree, usually on politics. Thanks, brother, not for sharing your views on the state of the union, but for the second shot at life.

"Maybe one person and their luggage at a time?" I suggest to the Besties. When they finally enter the apartment, more hugs and kisses, and the travel recap begins.

"I sat next to the friendliest Black man on the airplane. He was one of those Rasta-something people? You know, with the hair and the whole *look*. But so nice." Of course.

"Do you know what the train to Belgium is going to *cost* us? You won't believe how much." Of course, of course.

The Besties maneuver around the small but uber-tidy apartment, pre-furnished for long-term business renters with numerous colorful paintings of boobs positioned above gray statues of boobs. Sharing the Wi-Fi password with them means Mom doing verbal gymnastics, yelling: "It's letters and numbers, ready? Capital S. Okay, now numbers: three. Back over to letters: small c. Then, again, back to numbers ..." And so on. I love them madly, and especially when they are all together. Fuhgeddaboudit.

And maybe you think that means it was a good thing her friends are with her when we get the call—the wrong call. I don't. They have probably been at the apartment for a couple of hours when it happens. I'm on a video conference, working from my bedroom upstairs, when Bryan calls me. I guess he's been home from Berlin for a week at that point. I decline the call and shoot him a quick text: "On a work call - is it urgent?" He simply writes back: "Urgent."

I wish I hadn't called him back right away. You could have stayed a little longer.

"Dad died," he chokes into the phone. It sounds more like something you did, an activity. Dad golfed. Dad watched TV. Dad drank. Not something you were: dead.

My knees hit the hardwood floor. I think I keep telling him, "I can't catch my breath," over and over again. "You have to go tell Mom." *Fuck you, big brother. You tell her.*

At that point, I don't know much. I don't know that Bryan has to go to the house and, what(?), find you, identify you? *Who called him to tell him? The cops?*

I don't yet know that you have been found by co-workers when you don't show up to teach your Monday night class. Monday, July 23, 2018. Now I imagine they pull up to the house, see a car in the driveway, and think *Someone is home.* When no one answers the door, do they walk around the back of the house and see you, what? Lying on the kitchen floor? Do they assume they are in an urgent situation, thinking you can be revived? I don't even know who they are. I never ask.

"Mom, can you come upstairs?" I ask, trying to keep the shaking out of my voice. But she knows. She thought it when you didn't call. In that way you imagine something bad so that it *doesn't* happen. And when she hears me ask her to come upstairs, she *really* knows.

"Dad?" she simply asks before falling onto the bed. I only nod. Funny how you think a scene like this will play out. Uninformed me guesses Mom will crumble in silence. No. Her tiny frame falls onto the bed, and she starts punching it, screaming "No!" on repeat.

The rest is blurry. Who tells the Besties downstairs that you are gone? Is it me? Is it Mom? Even now, I say that you are "gone" or that you "passed." I rarely say *dead.* But you are dead. At this point, you have been dead one day.

I immediately try to book flights home. It's evening in Luxembourg. We can't fly out until the next day.

I cry on the phone to multiple airline reps, playing the death card. They don't believe me. They don't know I'm not that good of an actress.

Could I ever have a job where someone calls me crying "death," begging for help to get home, and I'm forced to follow company policies? No. This is why I have a bullshit paper-pushing legal job where the only thing that can die on my watch is a trademark.

I do remember making a potentially grave (pardon the pun) mistake. The Besties have just landed in a foreign country, and somewhere in all the torment, it's decided they'll stay in Luxembourg. I worry about leaving them in an unknown foreign city, even though it's really a town. They speak Long Island Expressway, not Luxembourgish.

Somehow, we convince Mom to get a shower, and I naively take the Besties for a walk down Boulevard Royal, the main artery, full of traffic, cafes, and imposing banks, so they can get their bearings. They keep asking me if I'm OK, and I keep answering in short, oddly chipper statements of being fine, mentally begging them to let me compartmentalize and play tour guide. *They must think I'm an emotionless zombie.* I am. We are probably 10 minutes into our numb walk when it strikes me: *Mom's alone. Will she try to hurt herself? How dumb am I to leave?* Other than her New York Italian emotional tendencies, nothing particular about Mom makes me think she would do anything, just that I don't know what a person's capable of in grief and in shock. I quickly turn back to the apartment, declaring the tour over. And for the size of Luxembourg, it really was.

Mom doesn't do it. You could say it was because she didn't have a gun, because the inner workings of an oven no longer allow for the Sylvia-Plath method, or because the Golden Gate Bridge wasn't nearby. But I don't think it was a lack of available tools or methods, simply that neither of us thought this hell was real.

By the time we land at home, you are two days gone. Funny how there's a lot I can't remember, but I remember that flight. There are no direct flights from Luxembourg to … well, anywhere that's not Europe. So, at the layover in Frankfurt, I am numb and can't figure out how to get us through customs and security to our connecting flight. Or did I even have to do that? Maybe we have to go through security a second time, in case we purchased a gun mid-air from Luxembourg? I remember running up to a ticket counter and begging the woman behind it to help us make our connection.

Time is standing still while it races by. We're maybe 20 minutes out from our flight taking off, waiting in a security line, snaking so far through the airport it feels like we are back outside on the curb. I've now cried to airline reps to find us flights, the cabbie to step on the petrol, the ticket agent to help us get through security, and security to help us get through security. I am never above crying to get my way, but I have run out of anyone receptive to my pleas.

Next up, the retired couple behind us in security strikes up a conversation with us (sadly for them) about the massive, glacial pace of the line. The wife shakes her bobbed hair in disgust, wearing her leather purse diagonally across her floral top; probably, a travel agent had cautioned them to protect their passports. The husband, cell phone on belt loop, stoops to pull his white socks up so high from his Nikes that I think: *Midwesterners*. Baby boomers might call them WASPs, but my generation doesn't talk like that. While I can't remember much of those 24 hours, these two I can't forget. They have been traveling to 10 or so European cities and are worried they are going to miss their connecting flight to: I didn't actually process anything they said.

"Where are you two ladies headed?" the wife innocently asks, making conversation. Word to the wise: Never ask an Italian New Yorker in crisis a question. *Any* question. They will answer you honestly.

"We need to get home to Philadelphia. I just found out my husband died. And they are making us wait in this security line, and we are going to miss our flight, and I am in a FUCKING NIGHTMARE," Mom says, her words tripping over each other to get out.

The woman immediately bursts into tears, which somehow feels helpful. The husband frantically starts flagging down every airport worker he sees. Something tells me he has success in life, flagging people down to get what he wants. He finds someone, somewhere, and is able to do the job I failed. He gets us through the line and onto our plane. I wonder if they remember us. Mom and I still think about them, although these days she also thinks about how lucky they are to have each other later in life—what she thinks every time she sees a gray-haired couple now.

I couldn't fly for a few years after that without having a flashback with a side of panic attack. Being on a plane put me right back on that flight home to you. I cried on flights for maybe two years. Not *sobbing* for Christ's sake, only tears rolling down my face. Nobody sitting next to me ever looked my way or asked if I was okay. That probably speaks a lot about our current society, but I'm grateful for that.

On this flight, I watch a Marvel movie over and over again, entering my fourth showing as we land. Mom is mostly silent, and I never ask what she's thinking, if she's OK, if she needs anything. She's thinking nightmarish thoughts, she's not OK, and I can give her nothing she needs. There's no point.

Bryan and Robyn pick us up. As we climb into the minivan, Mom sits shotgun, and she and Bryan start in on logistics: Where is Dad's body? What has been done so far? What is the next step? Who is at the house? Mom sounds eerily calm and matter-of-fact. Nothing like the woman who beat the bed, screamed, cried, or sat utterly mute for one day and two flights. In stark contrast, I lie across the van's back seat, head in my arms, and cry uncontrollably. It actually feels good. The sound of my sobs reaches the front of the minivan.

"Do you want us to stop talking?" Mom asks.

"Yes," I manage. We sit mostly in silence for the rest of the hour drive.

The next few days are random snippets. Your baby brother comes by with his whole family, and they sit around the kitchen island acting like you're dead. I walk out of the room, a move I perfected from you. Your big brother can't even come. His heart is broken, and he never did care about convention.

Flowers come to the house. Some are all white and make the living room look like somebody died. I throw them out still in their milk glass vases. I find your bottle of Bombay Sapphire in the fridge, wasn't hard; it was smack dab in the middle of the top shelf. I throw that out, too. Nuns you work with at the university come by and all sit on the living room sofa with Mom. Holding her hands, they speak in those hushed cerebral tones that are even more of a requisite for the job than that whole being married to God thing, informing her that, before she got home, they came and read you your last rites. This is *not* comforting news for Mom. Her only rule of following your wishes is that nothing religious is done. You were an agnostic (said you wanted to hedge your bets) who worked with nuns at a Catholic university. We can't fault them for doing their job. Voodoo, you would call it, so what does it matter?

Food comes. Mom can eat nothing, so I eat it all: Family-size portions of lasagna. Vats of corn chowder. An entire cheesecake in 72 hours. *Case of wine, anyone?* Nope, already finished that. I've never understood people who say they are too upset to eat. Pass it down. Mom doesn't eat and doesn't say much of anything, but when she does speak, it's with a conviction coming from somewhere other than her Catholic upbringing.

The whole family, now only Mom, Bryan, Robyn, and me, *which feels absurd*, are in the living room, as far away from all the casseroles as we can get. Restless, I'm sitting in your favorite chair, the one with the leg half chewed off by Sophie the Dog when she was a puppy, complete with the electric massage cushion you strapped to the back of it. It no longer runs, but the metal balls still put pressure points on my back.

"I don't know what to tell you. We always said when we died, we would be cremated and put in Melitta coffee cans," Mom says. "Dad in regular and me in decaf." It's the clearest thing I've heard from her in days. "That's the coffee we drink every day, and it's the only plan we ever made for this." She said this to your brother, who called to convince her of a funeral and burial. She said this to your lifelong friend from Catholic school, the priest, who called to convince her of a funeral and burial. She held firm to the only plan you two had made: a standing joke.

I was happy to have something to do, even if it was the most ridiculous and depressing errand I have ever and (I'm calling it now) will ever run. Home for maybe 48 hours, I find myself standing in the "Cereal/Tea/Coffee/Baking Needs" aisle of the Acme grocery store—*your* Acme, the one you went to on an almost daily basis like a European. The pharmacist knew your name. A pharmacist has never known my name if not reading it off a prescription. The bank teller inside the Acme knew you. I haven't been to a bank since they started closing at 2:00 p.m.

There I am, looking for a Melitta coffee tin container to put your ass in, I mean, to put your *ashes* in.

I'm staring at Acme's coffee choices so I can buy a tin to hand over to the funeral home. *Price check on urns in Aisle 4.*

But what size? The 11 oz. standard can size looks a bit small. And we both know you had to shop in the husky boys' section as a child. You *would* have shopped at Big and Tall as an adult, but coming in at 5'9" on a good day, you only fit half the bill. And now the fundamental question: *How much ash does one husky-but-short man create?*

One Big & Tall Man (minus the Tall part)

+ pair of 40x32 (*extremely* hard to find) Docker pants

+ 2XL button-down shirt

+ suspenders (wait, maybe a belt, neither?)

+ Docksiders (no socks, you never found a use for them)

_____

= Damn, I suck at math

I size up the jumbo 22 oz. can and decide on 2 large and 1 regular, just in case. This doesn't seem like the time to be frugal. The funeral home will tell me what we need; they're the experts on ashes by the ounce. Plus, I hear most caskets are more than $16.95, so I'm already feeling pretty thrifty on your purchase.

I bring the cans home and pour the grounds into gallon plastic baggies. While this is all completely absurd to begin with, mid-task, I somehow start to associate the coffee grounds with your ashes, since I am pouring them out of what is now your urn. I don't want to waste the coffee, but I also don't want to *drink* the coffee that was only purchased to make way for your ashes. *How many scoops of Dad do I use for eight cups? Nine heaping scoops: one scoop per cup and one extra for the pot. Ten scoops if you think Dad seems weak.*

I wash out the cans, and admittedly, they smell wonderful. You're welcome. I'm buying Mom's decaf cans *now*, before it matters. Getting Mom's coffin cans in advance is the same as how her Italian New Yorker family does it anyway. The minute they approach 60, they purchase burial plots to use as a fun destination to take their grandchildren to in the summers, so we can marvel at the beautiful location and their "view." Getting Mom's decaf can now seems like the culturally appropriate thing to do.

This should be easier. She hasn't eaten in days and was only a buck 20 to begin with. Mom's an 11 oz.

So, thanks for the abrupt exit, leaving us with the eternal *What Ifs*, and little to no instructions for your remains or the remainder of our lives.

Jesus Christ, I hear ya, Jen. But let me say a thing or two? Best way I can describe it: Early on in our marriage, when you were still a baby and we were now outnumbered with the three of you kids, your mother asked me, "What would you do if I died?"

My face lit up. "I would move home to my mother's house," I said.

"What about the children?" she asked.

"Shit, I forgot about them," I said. I had. To me, the idea of going back to being taken care of by my mother would be The Life. You see, I'm a mama's boy. You never really grow up, and then one day you're goddamn old. Like ballplayer Satchel Paige asked, "How old would you be if you didn't know how old you was?"

The honest answer to all this is that I didn't know. I didn't know I was dying any more than usual. Sure, I felt like complete shit on *that* day, but do you know how often I felt like shit in the back half of my life? All the time. We're talking AFib, chronic heart disease, gout, lungs never right, sleep apnea, sometimes blood thinners, and peeing all the time, on Lipitor for life. Add it up. For me, every day just kinda hurt. I was running on empty.

Whenever I woke up from my daytime naps, I sat on the side of the bed for a good while, letting my feet hang off, "(Sittin' On) the Dock of the Bay." Remember how you thought I mastered some kind of meditation, the slow rise and shine? Shit, I was trying to wake the fuck up. That body couldn't jump out of a

bed. You can point fingers if you want. I'll point a chubby one back at myself if it makes you feel better.

I always said life was like a shit sandwich. Some days you get all bread, some days you get all shit. But most days, you get both. As I got older, it was more shit than bread.

I didn't know it was coming then. The doctors even told you guys that it was heart failure. I went fast, immediately. Hell, I had just made a real sandwich. That's why I was sitting in the kitchen, about to eat the damn thing. Which, ironically, reminds me of one of my better lines:

If Mama Cass had given her ham sandwich to Karen Carpenter, they'd both still be alive.

And I'll tell you what, I did try. To diet, to move this Chubb Rock. You don't know how it feels. No, you don't know how it feels to be me.

Addiction is addiction, whether booze or drugs or food. Food was only one of mine. And damn, did your mother try. I'm still pissed about that time I asked her to get me ham and cheese from the Acme, and she refused. Came home with ingredients to make low-sodium soup. Tasted like fromunda cheese. She was always trying to hold back the sandwich from me—her Mama Cass. Then there was the time when I knew we had blueberry pie leftover from some cookout. When I went to find it, turned out she had given it to the goddamn neighbors. That, I can never forgive.

What you think of as a selfish way to live, I think of as independence. I've told you kids for years: "No forced marches." You've got agency. Life shouldn't be a series of forced marches. I'd rather die at 70 with my ham sandwich than at 85 with someone wiping my ass in a home. Marriage vows are to take care of your spouse in sickness and in health; I made no promise to take care of myself. I did what I could, but Warren Zevon already said it for me: "My Shit's Fucked Up."

I always knew I wasn't living too long.

Hell, what did I tell you when you showed me how to deposit a check just by taking a picture of the damn thing on your phone? "I've lived too long. I'm ready to die," I said.

Even my doctoral students, if I were their advisor, I'd tell them to hurry up and finish their dissertation so they could get their degree before I died. It was funny 'cause it was true. I instructed them: "If you're up there defending your dissertation in front of the committee and you see my legs start twitching, or if I keel over, just keep going." How much more warning could I give?

My mother always said, "There are worse things than death." Weren't you listening? You've got such hostility. But, kid, Seger sang it best:

> *When you've got a heartache, there ain't nothing you can do.*

> *Charlie knows. There ain't nothing you can do.*

So, when you're feeling good and pissed, play that music, that "Heavy Music."

2

"God only knows
what I'd be without you."

—The Beach Boys

Here I am by myself, but not alone, driving the 48 minutes to work, east over a mountain that's more of a hill, then south down a four-lane highway that snakes through all the money in Silicon Valley.

We talk when I'm driving or showering—places where there's space and time. When I'm alone, you can finally get in a word or two.

Car rides are the real quality time. We listen to music together, and I feel your irritation when I skip over Jackson Browne's "Doctor My Eyes." You put that in rotation too often.

In our post-mortem relationship, I get to pick the topics. So, what do I want to talk about? This week is my 10th wedding anniversary, and I want to chat about marriage and how that contract is playing out. You had some dark yet compelling advice for the institution: *Make as much as or more than your spouse, so you can leave them.* Let me add: "In case you need to" leave them. I think you forgot that part?

You're all wrong. I said, *"Don't* get married." Then, I said, "If you *do* get married, you need to make equal to or more than your husband." (Sure, you can add, "in case you need to" leave him.) And I stand by my advice; you have choices. One of 'em is: take my advice or don't. Another is *choosing* to be with your spouse. It shouldn't be that a person's stuck. Know how many friends I saw pay out the wazoo to get divorced? Others stayed in shitty marriages because they couldn't afford to get out. Life of forced marches. If my telling you to make more money screwed up the scales, well, in the words of the Rolling Stones: *"I could not foresee this thing happening to you."* Your mother and I … we got lucky, is all. We made it to the stage in marriage where our reading glasses were interchangeable. I never felt stuck, except maybe when my belly got too big, and I couldn't fit behind a steering wheel. Whatever you choose, don't forget what I said to Rusty after I walked you down the aisle: "No givebacks."

I'm not talking about givebacks. For 32 years. I subscribed to your initial "don't get married" advice. And your: "Why waste money on a wedding if it's every day that we're choosing to be with our spouses?" A ceremony didn't hold meaning for me, but it did for our grandparents of the Greatest Generation. And I didn't want to be middle-aged and still saying "my boyfriend." (Back then, I didn't realize it would make me feel younger.)

I'm glad Rusty and I had a backyard ceremony. I overpaid for a simple white sundress. You, whose wardrobe consisted of hand-me-downs and swag from country club tournaments, splurged on a purple plaid shirt from Costco, pairing it with your standard-issue golf windbreaker.

You walked me down a lawn aisle, while a friend's daughter played the Beach Boys' "God Only Knows" on a violin. After 10 years, I'm not wavering, but our wedding song was an honest way to start a marriage: "I may not always love you."

You've been married for a goddamn minute; take it easy. I loved your mother in a place where there's no space or time. I never wanted out. When I met your mother, she was a student teacher and had taken a role in Philadelphia to get a little freedom from her parents. She got an apartment with Ginny on 22nd and Walnut above a belly dancing bar. Now it's a Sunoco gas station.

I was a senior at St. Joe's, living with my parents outside the city. Desperate for substitute teachers, they let education students sign up, make a little money on the side. Mom was the student teacher, and I was the sub for that one day: March 19, 1968. The only day I ever subbed. At the end of the school day, I tried to get my courage up, and I asked her out.

On that first date, I recited the lyrics from Simon & Garfunkel's "For Emily, Whenever I May Find Her" and pretended I wrote it. Hook, line, and sinker. She had a boyfriend at the time, an Italian fella. To the dismay of her parents, she ditched that goombah for this Polish, Irish, English teacher. You're lucky she didn't marry him, or you'd be even hairier.

She did waiver, once, at a pretty crucial moment: the night before our wedding. You gotta remember, we were just kids: 21 and 22. We didn't have a pot to piss in. We were staying at your grandmother's house, the one I called the Bowling Ball. 'Course I only used that "term of endearment" behind her Italian ass. We were in separate rooms, of course. This was 1970. Same year the Carpenters came out with "We've Only Just Begun." Mom was in the room she grew up in, as pink as the '60s. I was in your Uncle Bob's old room; in a twin bed I couldn't fit in, even back when I was lean and solid everywhere. Middle of the night, I got a soft knock on my door, only heard it because I wasn't fully asleep yet. Agita from too many bowls of gnocchi at dinner. That shit can kill ya.

"Buddy?" your mother whispered anxiously, "I don't think I can do this." I was focused on my gut and trying to make sleep

happen, in that state where you can hold a conversation, but not remember what you said in the morning.

"Okay," I said simply. "You don't want to get married. No problem. It's okay. We won't get married. Nothing we can do in the middle of the night to cancel a ballroom and 200 people." I'm good at getting people to go back to sleep. Just tell 'em whatever the hell they wanna hear.

You're lucky your mother woke up fine the morning of our wedding, ready to commit, or else you wouldn't be here. Since I was still in the courting phase, I let her pick our wedding song. I honestly didn't think she'd pick Barbra Streisand, but that song didn't lie: "People who need people are the luckiest people in the world."

"Need" is a tough one—now let me get this out. I pick the topics. Women have been told (by the likes of you) that we can do it all: make the money, make the beds, make the babies. For me, the first two out of three ain't bad.

Does it matter that there's no longer any head of a household? Has a woman taking your advice made men obsolete? From what I can tell, not yet. Women are social creatures. We crave companionship. Dildos don't cuddle, yet. (*Who says "dildo" to their father? You must be so proud.*)

It's unclear to me what the poor male schmucks of my generation, "Xennial men," have been told. It definitely wasn't to make their beds. I blame their mothers. While we were told to go have it all (horseshit!), maybe men were vaguely told to man up, be a man, take it like a man? If so, it was only to have the rug (picked out and paid for by a woman) pulled out from under them.

I recently hit one of these snags, pretending that Rusty had a say, pretending I wasn't gonna do whatever the hell I wanted. Problem is, I took your advice, plus I have a law degree in man-ipulation.

I bought a 1974 Volkswagen Beetle. Like buying a record player when music is streamed, or paying $100 on eBay for a pit-stained, moth-eaten, "vintage" concert T-shirt; it's a purchase in lieu of a not-yet-invented time machine. My Midlife Car-sis is "surfer blue" with a bit of sparkle and a black interior. I've always imagined myself driving one of these classics down California's Pacific Coast Highway. Rusty, the protective spouse, can only imagine me driving *over the cliffs of* the PCH. (It happens more than you'd think. California rarely embraces the guardrail aesthetic.)

Today I'm driving my dependable Lexus to work, same one you took me to buy 13 years ago when I got a job outside of Philly and had my first commute. But getting the Bug like you owned back in the '70s feels like you're really with me in the car, even though you couldn't squeeze in this tin can. I can feel your eyes close as your pudgy hand pulls your temples together, creasing vertical lines in your forehead …

Are you telling me that you bought some classic car you don't need, and I'm guessing you can't drive, simply because I told you I happened to own a couple Beetles years before I put you on this Earth? Orange one and a yellow one. If this purchase is about me, can I suggest a sensible Pontiac instead? Maybe a wooden-paneled Dodge Caravan? We had lots of those. But a classic Beetle, engine in the rear and gas tank in the front? It's a goddamn death trap.

Congratulations: It was a three-way tie, but you just pulled ahead as my dumbest kid.

Don't worry, the prior owner added seatbelts, along with a tape deck. No power steering, no power brakes, and at the top of the list: You're right, I have no clue how to drive a stick-shift. So don't worry, I won't be driving the Bug on these California highways. She's meant for in-town, and of all four of her gears, she prefers 35 mph.

You weren't a car guy, but you're all I know of cars. I spent my childhood drives staring at the back of your rotund head, which seemed attached directly to your shoulders, no neck needed. Whenever I wanted you to change the station, stop for ice cream, or simply to curb my boredom, I'd wedge my kiddie feet in the velour crevasse where the backrest met the driver's seat and give you a little kick in the ass.

> **Yeah, but I got you back. I would tell you to duck back there as I rolled down the window to hawk loogies, your mother seated next to me, resigned to a mere "Buddy, please." I will say, the spark goes out a little when much of marriage is putting up with disgusting habits. Don't worry, though, what someone can put up with changes over time.**
>
>> ***Who do you*** *need* ***to annoy the shit out of you for the rest of your life? There's your definition of "need," and there's your spouse.***

In addition to your many demonstrations on how to loogie out a car window, you taught me to drive on a Sunday afternoon in a bank parking lot on the corner of Route 401 and Pottstown Pike, with "Jesus H. Christ" along for the ride, based on how you invoked his name. We drove your Chuck Berry-red Dodge Intrepid, a '90s version of a land yacht, with no particular place to go.

My Intrepid trepidation grew when I couldn't maneuver that boat into standard-width parking spots. The lot was particularly small since the little brick bank was once a house. The driving was low stakes on three sides, where missing the pavement only landed us in a cornfield. The lesson ended when I steered the car too close to the bank wall, smacking the side mirror into the vacuum tube that sucks up checks and spits out money. *Objects in the mirror are closer than they appear.*

The Beetle fulfills my warped sense of nostalgia for an era I didn't live through. I probably wouldn't have gone to Woodstock due to long lines, crowds, rain, and mud. Now, I live near that famous

California Rte. 1 and drive a classic Bug, reliving my non-existent hippie days. I used my bonus on this gas-guzzler that won't take me more than an hour south to Santa Cruz.

Rusty was initially against it. As I hatched my plan, his big hazel eyes grew three sizes, and his shoulders hit his ears in anxiety. He tried to shut it down, like what happens when you release the clutch too fast, shifting into first gear (did I get that right?).

Rusty's hypervigilant. It makes him great in an emergency (like when a parent dies) and a pain in my ass on a sleepy Sunday. His objections were sevenfold and fairly sound:

1. We don't know how to drive a stick shift.
2. We have two perfectly good automatic transmission cars.
3. We don't tinker.
4. We don't know how to change oil.
5. We don't know a mechanic who works on classic cars.
6. We don't know what insurance costs.
7. We don't even know how to buy a car from an individual.

There may have been more. I stopped listening. Whenever you stopped listening, you did us the courtesy of walking out of the room, physically moving on from the conversation. I tend to start looking at my phone. In this case, I was on Craigslist surfing for Beetle listings in a 50-mile radius.

Rusty couldn't even bring himself to car shop with me. But he hadn't factored in Bill, our neighbor. Bill's retired and about your age, or the age you would be. He lives alone and lost his wife six or so years ago, around the same time we lost you. Having Bill down the street provided me a solution that was sevenfold and fairly sound:

1. Bill taught all of his children how to drive a stick shift and offered to teach me.
2. Bill wanted to car shop, kick the tires.
3. Bill built and owned two Bugs back in the '70s, the definition of a "tinkerer."

4. Bill knows how to change oil.
5. Bill offered to drive the Bug up the Pacific Coast Highway to the classic car mechanic three towns north.
6. Bill asked the prior owners what insurance they use.
7. Bill simply googled how to buy a car from an individual, printed a bill of sale, and drove me in the Bug the hour back to our neighborhood. A Corvette driver threw us a peace sign as he blew past us on Rte. 101.

I named her Dolly Parton. Based on her year, she rolled off the lot around the same time as "Jolene" and "I Will Always Love You," which, legend has it, were written on the same day. Car's got talent (a good engine), plus voluptuous headlights.

When I first drove her, I stalled backing out of the driveway, around the neighborhood, at the stop sign. Then, the song "9 to 5" came on the radio, and I hit the brakes in excitement and stalled while "Waitin' for the day my ship'll come in."

Bill's nothing like you. He's a former engineer who's thoughtful about how things work, like the 3D printer in his garage. He keeps attempting to teach me the mechanics behind Dolly's engine. He never yells when I buck her into first gear and stall out onto the shoulder of Highway 1, traffic whizzing by.

> Bill simply says, "Oops, let's start again." Sometimes I wish he'd shout, "Sonofabitch, you're gonna kill us both."

As Rusty watches my driving lessons with Bill, he's making a comeback. He bought a book called *How to Keep Your Volkswagen Alive*, an engine belt, a fire extinguisher, and spark plugs, for some reason. He changed the oil and cut his garage woodshop in half to fit Dolly Parton.

A year later, and I still don't let on that I haven't figured out this stick-shift thing. I'm stalling out all over the place, stomach flipping as I roll down hills. I drive with the windows down even when it's cold out, so I can motion for cars behind to pass me. The other day, I thought I was in neutral, started her up, and crashed into the garage. If you tell Rusty *any* of this, you're a dead man.

Maybe I'm not very good at this marriage thing? I never bought into the idea of two becoming one. We're still each a person with our own dreams, no? I guess my question is: What if you love your spouse, but you don't need them to keep the roof over your head because you make money, to help you parent offspring 'cause you don't want any, to teach you to drive stick 'cause there's Bill, or to fix the toilet because Angie made a list?

You didn't know how to fix anything, but you handled it. You always said, "Just pay someone." Or more specifically: "Make money so you can pay someone to fix shit. Maybe flirt a bit if you have to." So, whose castle is it now?

These are my questions, and I've still got 22 minutes left in this commute.

Look, I don't know what it's like to go through life as a broad. But I'd still tell you the greatest union there ever was, what you should model your marriage after, is Mick Jagger and Keith Richards. Now they stuck for the right reasons, and it didn't look easy from the cheap seats. You know, Keith can sing, I mean, really wail.

The story goes that Keith was asked in an interview why he doesn't take lead vocals, why he's not the frontman. Legend has it he shot back, "What would Mick do?" That's love. That's ignoring the interviewer trying to drive a wedge in your union. And even if it's not true, how about the fact that they're still touring together? They can't *need* the money. All that talent? They're not stuck with each other. They could each rock alone. They *choose* to band together. Makes 'em all better.

In that Scorsese documentary, *Shine a Light*, some old interviewer asked Keith, "Who's the best guitarist, you or Ronnie?" Richards didn't miss a beat: "We're both lousy, but together we're better

than 10 others." Bullshit interviewer, tryin' to start him up. And don't get me wrong, it looked complicated to stay in a band. All the fucking drugs, booze, cigarettes, life on the road. It probably wasn't easy, but better. I still can't believe they outlived me. And those bastards kept all their hair.

Sounds like you think you don't need people. You know, both of my Beetles were stolen. First one was nabbed right out in front of our Glenmoore Apartments in Clifton Heights. Al, the mechanic across the street, watched the whole damn thing, but the thief came with a key, so Al thought it was one of my brothers. After that, I wised up and sold the second one to my brother, and then *that one* was stolen from him. So, listen to me, "Mick Jagger," don't act like you don't need people.

Marry the person you need to be with when you walk outside and realize your car is stolen. If you don't believe me, ask the Stones, cause "*… sometimes you just might find you get what you need.*"

"... *see, you can't please everyone* So *you got to please yourself.*"

—Rick Nelson

It's Sunday morning, and that doesn't mean church for this ex-Catholic you made in your image and after your likeness. My Sunday mornings, oh hell, Saturdays, too, I make a coffee and get back in bed. I worship coffee. I get it from Wawa, that mecca of a convenience store up and down the I-95 corridor. We don't have Wawas out West, so whenever I go home (meaning Pennsylvania, I don't think I'll ever call California "home"), I pack a suitcase full of my favorite roast: regular.

Just back from a visit East, I'm leaning on propped up pillows, sheets still warm from sleep, thinking about more of your advice, Dad. Not your warning to skip seeing Van Morrison live since all he does is perform each song exactly as recorded, and walk off stage without a word to the audience. (I didn't listen, and now I'm out $200.) And not the one about how to get four uses out of the same pair of underwear (move front to back, flip inside-out, repeat)—I'm still worried that was serious, something you learned once you retired and Mom stopped doing your laundry.

I mean, your advice not to have kids. You told me this my whole life. You said it to Robyn even after she *had* kids, an "I told you so" whenever it looked like motherhood was going to break her. Your voice was like your go-to candy, root beer barrels: bold, controlled, and sweet and spicy all at the same time.

I began repeating your mantra around age 15: "I'm not having kids." Since I carry a uterus with all the piping, no one believed me. "You'll want them one day," Mom would insist, often retelling the scene when, as a toddler sitting in her lap at Sunday Mass, I began to kiss her all over the face and wouldn't stop, everyone in the pew laughing at a display of more love than the Catholic church had ever shown them. Adorable, but I'm not sold.

You could have saved your breath with the "No Kids" advice because I had already formulated the plan. Or was that you already in my head? We may never know.

I told Rusty we shouldn't get married because people would start asking when we were going to have kids. He said they wouldn't, and he was right. They don't ask *him*. They only ask me.

Of course, I did question him about it in lawyerly fashion, early on in the relationship, giving myself the unilateral right to amend our contract.

"Do you want kids? I don't want kids. So, if you want kids, you should think about that. But also, I reserve the right to change my mind. You have no right to change your mind. So, think before you answer."

"Huh."

He casually considered this life-altering decision: "I just assumed it was something you do. Get a job, get married, have kids. A life without kids sounds kinda nice."

Ah, to be a man. A man who now has time for guiltless video games. He's in the den now, playing some game that, whenever I walk in to fill up another cup, looks like he's taking one long continuous walk in the woods without leaving the couch.

Finally, in my forties, with eggs drying up and small boobs sagging (Mom warned: "Even the small ones fly south for the winter of your life"), I thought folks would accept this decision, but still the questions come.

Like Dr. Pepper, I'm so misunderstood. When I told you, "Don't have kids," I was giving you more choices. You didn't hafta listen. Your brother and sister didn't. Why did you? For your mother and me, it's just what you did. If you wanted to do the horizontal bop, you got married. If you got married, you had kids. And Jeannie *needed* kids. She was wired to give everything and then more. Maybe that's motherhood?

That '70s birth control was mighty strong, couldn't get it outta her system. Took us years to have your brother. Of course, it was your mother who needed three. She wanted a house of chaos, like your sister made with her four slobs. You? You're built like me; our nerves can't handle it. For my generation, it just was. For you, it could be: Have a career without worrying about mouths to feed. Move around without worrying about school districts. Make life a little easier. Ever hear of a D.I.N.K.? Double income, no kids? Sounded neat to me.

Travel. You forgot it's also easier to travel.

That's right, I coulda been a travelin' man, but with kids, we couldn't afford that. I left the States once in my whole life. In '97, a group of us went to Scotland for our 50th birthdays. If this ain't heaven, then St. Andrews is. I stood on that famous bridge between the 1st and 18th fairways, and I stayed at the nicest hotel I'd ever seen, The Jurys, right in downtown Edinburgh. You know I love a good hotel lobby, the people watching, the coming and going. I found a couch right in the middle, kicked off my loafers, propped my bare feet up on the coffee table, and settled in.

"Yo, Bud, for real?" My brother Bob, the world traveler, disgusted as he returned from checking us in. Lucky for him, my gout wasn't swelling at the time. On our last day, I may or may not have checked out wearing only the bathrobe from the room. Turns out that trip was a once-in-a-lifetime; I never left the country again.

Well, West Coast to East Coast travel is starting to feel like another country. This time, I was back East for Mother's Day, trying to find a non-depressing holiday to celebrate without you. While I was visiting home, I met my childhood friends for dinner. You'll remember them as *The One Down the Street*, or *The Tall Blonde One*.

As we ordered wine and settled into dinner, the catching up began. "Remind me how old the kids are now and what grades they're in?" They recounted their latest parenting stories, who's playing what sport, who missed the bus, how the oldest wants a phone. I responded with my childhood stories ("I was scared to miss the bus too!") even though I think you're supposed to use your own kids—not yourself—to compare against.

Rusty constantly warns me, driving back from social situations, eyes growing big but still on the road, head shaking side to side, "Dude, you can't interject stories of our dog when people talk about their kids."

"All I said was that Rosie's having the hardest time at daycare because she hates having her butt sniffed. It's true," I say side-mouthed and proud.

The most interesting story at that girlfriends' reunion dinner was how early sex ed is taught, and how clinical it is. Based on what I have now learned *they* are learning, I don't think I could label a diagram of this plumbing of mine that dictates how the world perceives me. *Do I have a vas deferens, or does the guy?* You didn't tell me they would pity me as the woman who doesn't know *true love*, the love of a child.

I've been around my nieces and nephews enough, and once even attended a "Mommy and Me" class when Robyn couldn't.

"Isn't this adorable?" A mom next to me shrugged her shoulders up with an expectant look. Moving my eyes away from the clock, I looked at my two non-participant nephews standing against the wall, staring down at their shoes because they couldn't yet read time. My eyes darted to the group of kids missing every basket they threw, then over to the ones doing somersaults that looked more like the worm. I've never wished time away faster. "A-dorable," I said, hoping she wouldn't figure out the two non-participant pants-wetters were technically "mine" in this scenario.

I hear these women say they weren't whole until they had children, but I can't picture it, don't know what it means. I never knew I was less than all of me.

"Who's my favorite person to hang out with?" I constantly quiz Rusty when I'm couch-bound on a Saturday night. "Yourself." He's perfected our call and response and need not look up from his phone.

We had a call and response, too, remember? "Why did I have Bryan and Robyn?" "To get to me!" you'd yell. Although to keep you guessing, in your teenage years, I'd also ask: "Why did I have you? I already had one of each flavor."

This got modified when I became Buddy Pop, a grandparent.

"Who's my favorite grandkid?" I constantly quizzed any one of them who came over to eat me out of house and home. "The one who's not here," they all knew to answer in unison, slyly smiling up at me, hoping I'd unwad my cash and throw some their way for a job well done.

You can't mourn what you don't know to miss. All I know is the love of my dog and husband. (Turns out we are DINKWADs: <u>D</u>ouble <u>I</u>ncome <u>N</u>o <u>K</u>ids <u>W</u>ith <u>A</u> <u>D</u>og.)

I try to picture what I'm missing. I imagine someone who's never heard music. My heart would ache for them. I couldn't describe music, or what it does down to your bones. Maybe it's all the love and pain in that magical medium. But music never rips open your vagina, pukes on you, or tells you in a fit of hormonal rage that you ruined its life.

The real shock isn't that I ran out of things in common with some friends, it's how gradually it happened. Like your insistence on special ordering a flip phone long after smartphones came around, the connections in these friendships are becoming harder to find and not as useful for any of us.

It wasn't right when the first baby was born, but they didn't seem to mind that I avoided holding it. Holding babies makes my arms go numb, and there's no clear social guidance on when to give them back. About 20 seconds in, you'll hear me say, "I have to pee." It's the only way out. Once these offspring became people, the shift started. These friends, we helped shape each other, but we're not doing that anymore. I miss them as kids; now they are moms.

I liked it best when you all became *people*. My favorite time of life was empty nesting—finally, a little peace and quiet. I was 34 when I had you and only 52 (still a baby) when you went off to college, but, God, I felt old. I was sad to see you go, only because I knew what college costs. And when we finally had that empty nest, it was your mother who was empty. Her last lovey bird. Considering her dread, she did pretty well when we dropped you off in the middle of Pennsylvania. The drive home was a straight shot, three hours on the turnpike, mostly in silence except for my radio surfing, back to a still house.

The day after, as we got in the car to go to breakfast, KYW News Radio on for *Traffic & Transit on the Twos*, a house of vacant bedrooms, and only the dog to skutch us, I tried on an optimistic tone for her.

"Day one wasn't so bad," I managed, as one of my coughing jags started, and I maneuvered the car seat back and the steering wheel up—not for my height but for my belly.

"Your giant belly is crushing your lungs," she retorted.

"Day two isn't starting out so well." I stared ahead.

Midway through my East Coast reunion dinner, I brought up midlife and how my forties feel like a natural point to pause, deconstruct my life choices, and maybe write a review.

"Do you regret not having kids?" one friend asked too quickly, eyes on her wine, hands playing with the stem of the glass.

"No, but I feel like if I'm not doing that with my life, shouldn't I be curing cancer or something?" Elbows on the table, I turned my hands up to the heavens like my Italian heritage taught me to talk. This is my go-to response. I lean into the assumption that my life is as empty as my uterus, instead of saying, "I freaking love my life. Some mornings I get back in bed with coffee, a book, and a big freaking smile on my face. But I'm human, so I still question my choices."

The conversation then turned to our laugh lines, forehead furrows, and those angry "elevens" between the eyes, which of them has gotten Botox, and if it works. My forehead wrinkles as I balk at the cost and wonder if these injections are done for your partner, your reflection in the mirror, or for other women. I'm the only one who let her hair go gray, wishing to look older so I may finally stop getting The Question.

After all these years, when I get The *Next* Question: "So why didn't you have kids?" I still don't have a socially appropriate *why*. I deflect with: "I'm really selfish," "I like naps," and "I wanna go to the movies." The truth is squishy, gray like my hair.

When I picture motherhood, I feel claustrophobic, stuck in a house full of plastic (plastic bottles, plastic swings, plastic toys), and I'm not allowed to leave. And when these babies grow out of their plastic cocoons, then they're kids talking back to me. And when they're done talking back, they need money for college. And after college, they move away. Damn those Cats and their Cradles.

I hate that you let your hair go gray. Makes me feel so damn old. And hell, yes, kids'll cost ya, and not only college, even your swear jar where f-bombs cost me $1 a curse. Some nights, I'd come home late after a long commute, release the rubber band holding my wad of cash together, and put a preemptive $20 in the jar to get through the night. Why was my money clip a rubber band? Two-fold: Kids require a quick-release system because you're reaching in it so often, and you're reaching in it so often that you can't afford a real money clip.

Besides the money, kids are painful. You love 'em so damn much it hurts. At the same time, you wish you could smack the shit out of them. In that way, there's nothing else like it. You kids did a real number on my nerves. Years of agita. Some of it from cardiomyopathy, some of it from copious bowls of gnocchi, most of it from you gonifs.

And I sure as shit couldn't handle when you got injured. With my heart, I was already living a bit dizzy and tired, short on breath. When your sister, the only allergic one, got stung from a bees' nest in the ground, those heart palpitations quickened. Who knew bees were even *in* the ground? As she screamed in pain, running through the backyard, I screamed back in parental pain, following as she ran to your mother. "What were you doing in the woods? Why would you step on a bees' nest? Don't you look where you're walking?" I yelled us to the E.R. I think that started my AFib.

You all were a pain in my ass that caused a pain in my heart.

See, Robyn ran to *Mom*. The kid always goes to the mom, not the dad. The mom is double duty. Which is why, in my imaginary parenthood state, I instantly hate my husband, who, in reality, I love. When I picture motherhood, I've decided he's lazy, isn't contributing enough, and the little he *is* contributing, he's doing wrong. In Imaginary Motherhood, I'm alone, screaming in my now-minivan-car parked outside my plastic prison because I can't go too far in case someone needs me.

> **You're right that your mother was the primary parent. Did you hear that? You're *right*. And lucky for me, kids remember every little thing as if it happened only yesterday, so they can hold it against you for fucking eternity.**

I don't want to be a mother. If anything, I want to be a father. I could do the parenthood thing if I had a wife. A wife remembers where the other sock is, which one doesn't like tomatoes, and how to calm those bastards down in the middle of the cereal aisle. And I mean a *wife*. I don't mean one of those modern, plugged-in, doting dads. From what I can tell, even they still don't know kids' doctors' appointments, who their playgroup friends are (and aren't), or if it's time for a new winter coat.

I want to be a father in the '50s, or hell, even the '80s, like you. I want to come home from a day at the office, loosen my tie, release a giant belch, and kick off my Docksiders while flopping on the couch, only to have offspring come rub my thick neck with their tiny kid hands. And I want to say things like: "Go ask your mother." I don't see the kids crying for *dad*. I hate the idea of being needed *that* much as a mom.

> *You didn't show me how to navigate this world as a woman; you taught me how to be you.*

The last gift I ever gave you was a mug with the saying: "Dad: Thank you for teaching me how to be a man, even though I'm your daughter."

Maybe that's why I wore neckties in the '90s. Or maybe it was because Madonna was doing it.

You wanna be a father? Well, for me, that meant worry. And probably was the same for the rest of us '80s dads loosening our ties. Sure, there was no equal division of anything back then. But the breadwinner title was a different stress. And look, how the hell would I know what it's like to be a broad and not have kids? Without kids, I probably woulda stayed a teacher instead of having to move up to school administration for the paycheck. Maybe I woulda bartended in the summers. "Wasting away in Margaritaville," as they say …

Instead, I spent my summers going into debt for our yearly Carolina vacation, piled in a minivan, my right ass cheek numb for the 10-hour drive south down I-95. We left at 4:00 a.m., not to avoid beach traffic like I told you, but because I wanted you slobs asleep for the drive. "Are we there yet?" "I have to pee." "I'm hungry. Can we stop at Shoney's?"

When you were hungry, I played Jimmy Buffett's "Cheeseburger in Paradise" on cassette, hoping to change your attitudes while we changed our latitudes. I invented car games to shut you all up. One point if you saw a dead animal on the side of the road. No points if you saw a shoe. But if you saw the *matching* shoe down the road a piece, then you won the game. One point per Baptist church. But if you saw a *synagogue* as we entered the South, then you won the whole goddamn thing. That game ended in 1996 on Highway 17 near Sneads Ferry with a pair of Chucks 50 yards apart. Most of parenting is trying to get time to go by, but then it does.

It was Robyn who won the game with the matching shoes. Now back to my ladies' dinner. Toward the end of it, the conversation turned to ridiculing husbands: Which one needs detailed operating instructions to function as a B- parent, why the preferred Dad Sport is a 4-hour round of golf followed by a "mandatory" lunch instead of a 30-minute pickup basketball game. I didn't need offspring to enjoy these truths.

As we did a round of goodbyes outside the restaurant and I embraced my oldest friends, the ones who drove me to high school, who dedicated their teenage years to acquiring shitty weed to share, and who would never tolerate anyone outside our click ridiculing us, I wondered if having history in common would be enough.

I misunderstood your favorite last line from *Stand By Me*: "I never had any friends later on like the ones I had when I was twelve. Jesus, does anyone?" I thought I would keep my closest friends *forever*. But now I know that there'll never be another moment in time when I have a group of friends like this.

I can't give you any other reason to have or not have kids, except if I didn't have kids, who'd be talking to me now? Although peace and quiet sound nice, too.

Shit, if you have regrets, you can *do* the parent thing, but you can't *try* it. You can try jobs, houses, partners, diets, drugs, but not kids. You sound like you don't know what you want. As a parent, you're expected to know stuff—how the world works. Do *you* know how the world works? Yeah, me neither. I didn't know there'd be the distance with your girlfriends.

So, sip your coffee in bed, and remember one of my most important lessons: You can pick your friends and you can pick your nose, but you can't pick your friend's nose. Respect their choices, too. My other advice: no forced marches.

4

"Workin' too hard can give you a heart attack-ack-ack-ack-ack-ack."

— Billy Joel

I'm driving home from work to my teaching job when Mom and Robyn call to rehash a meeting with that medium in their town, the one we've gone to before, trying to get to you. Well, to be specific, in case you are omnipresent and watching us. Mom called, and I did the 'ol Add Call/Merge Call to patch in Robyn.

It's important to get all perspectives at once when it comes to calls from beyond.

Maybe it's a waste of money since you live in our heads, but this medium is always pretty spot-on.

Mom rationalized, "Maybe she's reading our minds?" Even that's a cool party trick and worth the money. At the end of this session, Mom asked about me, "What about my other daughter? Does he have anything to say about the one who doesn't live here?"

"Oh, he says she hates her job," the medium apologized. Is that advice from the beyond? What am I supposed to do with that? Now I, too, think she's mind-reading. She seems to know that I still don't know what I want to be when I grow up. You suggested law school. "Everyone goes to college these days; you gotta keep goin'. Get another degree," you told me.

I also told you to get a bullshit undergraduate degree in "thumb up your ass" so your GPA would be high enough to get into a law school.

Yes, so I majored in Communications (✓), which got me a high GPA for law school (✓✓), which got me a nice mound of debt (–).

And when I asked how much debt you racked up for undergrad plus law school, do you remember your shit-for-brains answer?

I believe my math and your parenting skills gave me the answer:

"Uh, I have about $100,000 of debt. Some of my interest rates are low, maybe 2%, but others are high, around 8%. Let's say an average 5% interest. So, 5% of $100,000 means I owe $105,000."

You closed your newspaper so I could see your disgust: eyes narrowed, nose crinkled, upper lip curled, jaw tightened like someone asked you to eat the shit you were hearing.

I had to slow my response for you, realizing my 25-year-old was still a child: "No, you owe 5% *over 20 years*. So, $5,000 times 20 years is another $100,000. You owe $200,000. It's *simple* interest. Why did you think someone would loan you $100,000 and only want $5,000 on their investment?"

"Because they're the government and they want me to get a good education.?" I answered-asked. "Are you saying my education cost twice what I paid for it?" *Slowly recalculating what I paid for weed.*

I still can't believe you earned multiple degrees. You should give them back.

Now what? I tracked time billing in 6-minute increments for years at a law firm to put a dent in those loans (✓). I went to work at a company, hoping for better hours with no timesheets (✓✓). But you didn't tell me how goddamn boring it would all be.

I thought that extra degree would *mean something*—not the way I'm using it. I earned a piece of paper to hang on the wall next to my other piece of paper to let me push more paper. The only time I've been to court was traffic court in Philly. And that was merely a cubicle visit in some government building when I racked up over $300 worth of tickets for parking my scooter on the sidewalk.

I'm a fine-print poet. My job is to advise: "Can we add the word 'approximately' so as not to guarantee a delivery time?" I get paid to keep those lawsuits away. Sometimes I hate myself when the job forces me to say things like "so as" and "for the avoidance of doubt."

> *Based on my current skill set, if you had a tombstone, I would have edited it to read:*
>
> *"Died <u>on or about</u> July 23, 2018."*

You're making this all too hard. Let me ask you this: How much are you making these days? Ballpark, *before* taxes. The job isn't pointless. The *point* of the job is to make money. There's your point.

The pay is good, bordering on great. The people are courteous, bordering on nice. You told me to get a high GPA and get a second degree, but you never told me how to have a career in something I'm passionate about. How much of this life have I spent in silence, staring at a contract, deciding between writing "and" or "or" or "and/or"? With that $100,000 law school diploma (wait, $200,000), I understand the cost of contract drafting gone wrong—I just don't care. I've based my career off the saying printed on your favorite coffee mug: "If you can't dazzle them with brilliance, then baffle them with bullshit."

Good God, "passion?" Cut the crap. That's naive bullshit your generation loves. Are you my kid? There's only two things: work and play. Work your ass off at something, then enjoy life, then back to work. Get up and do it again.

The acting I do from my cubicle at least deserves a role in community theater. In meetings, I often have to turn you off in my head for fear I'll call someone a prick or their idea "a perfectly tapered turd." I honed my acting craft by imagining your school board meetings, back when you were superintendent. How painful you said those were. I never knew you to keep your mouth shut at home, so how did you do it there?

Work, career, job—it's all a game. The trick is to never play the game too long.

When you were maybe seven or eight, as I walked in the door from work (after sitting in the driveway, listening to a few more tunes in that leased Dodge), you took my briefcase from me and, tripping over it, asked me, "What do you *do* at work?" The easy answer would have been to tell you I was a teacher. Probably the one job you could understand. But I was a public school superintendent, and I'm not about lying to my kids.

"I eat shit for a living."

"What?" you asked, as your eyes lit up in anticipation of money for your swear jar.

"No, wait. That's not exactly right. I take the shit I eat, and then I process it into new shit, and give it back. How do you like your shit? Sausage links? Shit patties? Here you go." At 25 cents a "shit," you just made a buck 25 for the jar: That's a pretty good job right there.

Yeah, but "fucks" were $1 each ... I was always waiting for an f-bomb.

School board meetings were the height of shit-eating. I would throw up before them—don't tell your mother. On the plus side, my office had its own bathroom and a couch for after-lunch naps on school board meeting days. How could a thing be so pressure-inducing that you throw up and yet so boring that you doze off? Budget monotony was only ever broken up by angry parents yelling. I'd take the boredom over the politics. Not good for the heart.

I didn't give a rat's ass about most of the pressure. But some of it was critical; there were kids on the other end of these decisions. Do I wish I had remained a teacher all those years and not gone into administration? Sure, but life's expensive. For teachers, a "career path" is away from kids and into administration. Take someone good with kids and promote them until they never see kids again. All they see and hear is bullshit parents.

When you're in administration, you're involved with two types of parents:

1. The ones who don't give a shit about their kids. (This one breaks your heart.)

2. The ones convinced that their kids are gifted and you're not challenging them enough. (This one breaks your balls.)

In board meetings, I had to learn to answer by saying *nothing*. You can't sling shit back and keep your job. All you can do is eat it. A public school board meeting means answering to the crowd of parents, taxpayers, and community members with nothing better to do on a Tuesday. They act like a mob, but instead of pitchforks and torches, they brandish test scores and tax bills. You can never say what you really think. Well, you can say it once, but then you're out.

"Why are our test scores declining year over year?" a parental mobster would spit.

"Because the Jewish families are leaving in droves and taking all the good test scores with them!" It was the truth. Instead: "We're looking into that. And we're working within the No Child Left Behind testing requirements." I ate the shit and formed it into a policy patty.

Hurt my heart to suppress the truth. As Jackson Browne sang: "[We] started out so young and strong only to surrender." I set out to teach and ended up eating shit instead. I was *The Pretender*.

Wait, hold on, I missed my turn off the highway, listening to you ... Google Maps wasn't paying attention to you, but I was, so now it's recalculating another 12 minutes to the campus, as I wonder, *What happens if the professor is late*?

Now I know for a fact you didn't *always* keep your mouth shut at work. One year, on "Take Your Daughter to Work Day" (yes, back in the '90s when they were still only bringing *daughters* to work because we stupidly thought *that* could break that plexiglass ceiling), waiting for coffee from a side table in the conference room, you asked the Black woman in line in front of us, "So how come Black people are such good singers?" I was 11. I knew to be mortified. In the '90s, we were progressively and wrongly taught that the country was a melting pot and that you shouldn't see or say race. My kid brain fired up:

Thought 1: DAD! You *can't* ask that!
Thought 2: At least say *African American*.
Thought 3: But, yeah, *great* question. Why are they such good singers?

The woman gave you a look and a (forced?) chuckle. Today, you might be canned.

You're right. Even with my secretary, Mrs. Hermann, I might not survive today. I can say "secretary" because this was back when we said, "secretary." She was my *secretary*, and she was a pitbull. I was too old to learn new words and new technology

for that matter. If it weren't for her, I would have been forced into early retirement *even earlier*. How many years did we work together—15? For all those years, I was a kept man. Mrs. Hermann was the wall they'd have to scale to get to me. Was she good at her job? Hell no. She was utterly disorganized, but she didn't look it. She was tall, probably had a good six inches on me. Black rimmed glasses, gray hair in a low bun. I should have asked her to put a pencil in that bun to really ham it up. This look kept 'em away. And that is priceless when you are a professional Shit Eater.

Once email became a thing, Mrs. Hermann printed out every message I received and left copies on my desk. I would write out a response on the paper, and she would send it out as if it came from me. No one ever knew. There was only one Mrs. Hermann.

I've never called a coworker by their last name. All those years I heard about Mrs. Hermann, I never heard you use her first name. Did you even know it?

Okay, Smart Mouth, it was Carol. But I called her "Mrs. Hermann" because she insisted on calling me "Dr. Stefanski." I tried so many times to get her to call me Bud, or hell, even Dr. Bud. She refused. So, I had to call her Mrs. Hermann 'cause you know the rule: Always match titles; everyone's the same. And don't forget my somewhat lesser-known rule: If you want coworkers to like you, bring donuts to the office. People are simple, like interest.

But with this internet thing, there's shit even donuts can't fix. I used to get bomb threats called in every now and then. They were full of it, just wanted school to close. Can you blame them? I'd answer: "I dare you" and then hang up. This was before Columbine. Before metal detectors marked school entrances. I couldn't do that job today, couldn't keep up. Fifteen years as a superintendent is a goddamn marathon. And the only race I won in my whole life was the same as everyone else: as a sperm.

But you stayed in the race, you left to teach college and—

I didn't leave. I was pushed out. That one time I said the truth and, fuck …

Okay, then you were *pushed* to teach college. But you told me it was the best job you ever had.

Well yeah, going from answering to a school board to 20-hour weeks at a college? I was practically a lounge lizard.

These last few years, I've been trying to transform the law thing into teaching, starting with an adjunct gig. Do you remember me asking you for advice?

"I applied for an adjunct job teaching at one of the law schools here," I called to tell you.

"Why?" you sighed.

"Because I have a passion for teaching," I declared. You snorted.

"You won't make any money. Don't leave law; you paid too much to get there."

"I'm not quitting my job to teach, but maybe one day. If you do what you love, the money will follow." Look at me, giving my first lesson.

"Not in academia." By this point, you were snot-laughing.

From what I saw, you always wanted to be a teacher but forgot to *stay* a teacher. You'd been an adjunct for years while superintendent of schools. When you were, let's say, *guided into retirement* and became a full-time professor, it seemed poetic. You ended where you started.

You're crazier than a shithouse rat. It wasn't some altruistic pursuit that had me taking adjunct gigs *on top of my day job*.

I had to pay for Christmas, three teenagers, vacations. And those doctoral programs I taught were full of ex-lawyers-turned-teachers-turning-principals.

Is this you quitting law? All I can say is, don't go teaching for the money. I wanted to be a teacher. I liked to listen to myself talk. Most of the guys I started teaching with back in the '70s were doing it, hoping to defer the draft. Once Vietnam ended, so did their teaching careers. I stayed a teacher, so using your vocabulary, I guess I had a "passion" for it.

Well, the university offered me the job two months after you died. I almost didn't take it. What was the point of teaching without you? And how do you create a syllabus? You were supposed to teach me how to teach. The fear I might not get another chance outweighed the fear of teaching without you. Plus, like you, I love to hear myself talk.

In the interview, did they ask you how you eat your corn on the cob? My favorite question—tells you a lot about a person.

No, but I eat it in circles. So, why am I doing this when I don't have to pay for Santa or braces? I guess I want these law students to see a professor who's not in a tweed jacket carrying some thick treatise. Someone who can't dazzle them with brilliance. I figure if they see me up there, they'll realize: *If she can do it, I can do it. Hell, anyone can do it.* And then they won't take themselves so damn seriously. That's my contribution to the legal profession.

Students constantly ask me how I got my job, how to get a job, and can I help them find a job. They never ask if I like the job. They assume the degree has status, and so the job must have purpose. I wouldn't lie if they did ask; I'm not that good of an actress. Although maybe for them, it will be a passion.

Jesus, again with the passion crap. Just bring your students donuts.

5

"*People* **who need people** ..."

—Barbra Streisand

Sitting on the cold bathroom floor, I gingerly pour nail polish remover on some balled-up toilet paper, feeling put out when it mostly disintegrates the paper as it always does. I've ruined enough carpet and hardwood through the years to know that bathroom tile is my only friend when it comes to DIY nails.

Staring at your flat Polish feet attached to my ankles, I scrub away the faded, chipped, deep-sea-green color named *The Perfect Cover Up*. My short piggy toes look chalky, dry, and naked as I file them with an emery board I took from my Nani Lil. I apply a pale pink *Ballet Slippers,* calling to mind her 1960s bathroom tiles. If I wanted to honor her even more, I would get my hair set, too.

Speaking of *The Perfect Cover Up*, here's the story of how we—you and me, Dad—killed Nani. I'm pretty proud of us. It'd be nice to know that you're proud, too. I mean, I didn't *know* if what we did would kill her. But I hoped it would. Even recovering Catholics like a confessional.

Back when you were still here, your mother-in-law, my Nani Lil (nicknamed Nani Little), had reached that point in life where people lie about their age in the other direction.

Nani Lil, never without painted nails and a spare rouge in the handbag, took me to get the "Rachel" haircut in the '90s, and later in life, often asked me to brush hair over her bald spot. She was somewhere in her eighties when she started rounding up, setting a compliment trap for whoever asked her age, forcing them to say, "Oh, my goodness, you look incredible for (pick a number: 85, 88, 90, 94, 98, 99, and finally 100)." Only we know that on paper, she didn't *quite* make it to 100.

Does anyone plan to live to 100? Since I have her generous Italian ass, I think I'd better. Each year, as she got closer and closer to that centennial birthday, she was keeping her marbles but burning through her cash. We moved her from the assisted living place you knew. Her new place wasn't fancy, but it was cheaper, yet somehow smelled better, and the food was a step up.

Around her mid-nineties, she announced that she wanted to live to 100. It sounded great as long as we didn't count up the dollars left in her bank to keep paying for this life, or how many of her friends were left, so she wouldn't be alone. The new place didn't take Medicare, so once the money was gone, this meant another move. Either somewhere sadder, or in with Mom, who would then spend her "golden years" taking care of others.

At one point, Robyn offered a solution: "Why can't we all just chip in? You, me, Bryan, and Mom. How much could it be? A few hundred each a month?"

"It's $6,000 a month. This isn't a cell phone bill," I smart-mouthed.

Family perspective's a funny thing. Nani still saw her daughter as young and spry, able to get Nan's Italian ass in and out of cars, through all the waiting rooms of all the doctors and dentists, capable of filling out mounds of VA paperwork to fight for money owed, to mediate complaints from The Home when Nani got too heated at bingo, threw food at the dining table in disgust at the quality, or told another resident they had a "cookie ass," whatever that means. The roles of mother and daughter had long been reversed.

I'll never understand how the same person can be such a different mother and grandmother. Isn't it all "mothering?" As a mother, Nani was a meatball of anxiety, quick to go off the rails. As a mother-in-law, according to you, a real crunt. But as a grandmother, she was a spunky devil-angel who overfed me while constantly telling me I was perfect.

Second-generation "off the boat," she managed to work into most conversations, along with the fact that she was a proud Italian. She once cornered a landlord of mine coming down the hallway of our brownstone and proclaimed, "You can't beat the Italians."

"Sure," he graciously answered, "except in World War II." At that moment, the look on her face was pure New Yorker—*I might be wrong, but I will never be in doubt.* The rest of her time, she was **an Italian**.

That's why my in-laws never approved of me. I'm not Italian. I'm not always talking about my next meal. I did have the Catholic thing going for me, got all those voodoo sacraments. Her parents wanted her to marry anyone else, provided he was Italian, Catholic, made good money, lived on Long Island, bought her jewelry for every occasion, and acted like her shit didn't stink. Instead, here I came: Polish-English-Irish mongrel, recovering Catholic, working as a teacher, and "stealing" her away from them. God forbid I take her all the way from Long Island to far-off Pennsylvania.

It was good we moved away, always drama with them, some family member or another, always on the outs. With those people, you're like a penis. You're in, you're out, you're in again. I was rarely in.

Sure, my in-laws liked that I picked up the tab at dinners. Whenever the check came, they suddenly had alligator arms. But your grandmother, she always said I was lazy. I wasn't lazy, I just didn't look or act like them.

Real laziness is shitting the bed and pushing it down with your feet.

Your grandmother hated that I didn't dote on your mother. It's not just that I didn't hold Jeannie's handbag when she shopped, I never even went shopping. Tough shit; that's not me, not how we were raised.

I didn't compliment her hair because I never *noticed* hair. Your mom had great legs, though. Your mom and me, we liked to tell people our wedding song was "Yellow Submarine," just for the blank stares. But it was really Barbra Streisand's "People." "People who need people are the luckiest people in the world."

But without you, she wouldn't have me as a granddaughter. Didn't that ever factor in? Before I became a too-cool-for-school teenager, you and Mom would send me to stay with her and Pop-Pop on Long Island for two weeks every summer. That's when she taught me to love the fact that I was Italian—even if only 50% of me—in that way that Americans grasp at heritage to make up for a lack of culture. Like the T-shirts your Uncle Joe Stefanski bought us as kids: "Kiss Me I'm a Quarter Polish."

The stereo in Nani's kitchen was always on, and the kitchen itself was almost always "on," something good cooking until the nighttime ice cream we'd eat in the back bedroom-turned-TV-room. We ate constantly until the lights went out and a formal announcement was made: "Kitchen is closed." Each trip, I would count the grandkid pictures on the refrigerator, making sure I was featured in more than, or at least equal to, Robyn and Bryan.

The stereo played the Rat Pack fairly exclusively, but Barbra Streisand and certain Italian singers were granted exceptions. Nani taught me that Dean Martin only spoke Italian when he was young and had to drop his Dino Paul Crocetti name for fame. Each time Sinatra came on, Nani pointed out that Pop-Pop was a blue-eyed Italian "… like Sinatra." When she played Italian music, she translated while she cooked.

"He's saying he loves her bunny," she motioned to her crotch with her hands full of eggy breadcrumbs for fried chicken cutlets. I don't know if Italian music is *that* pornographic, or if Nani's translation was a bit off since she only spoke a dialect.

Say what you want about the Italians, even with their own children, they're never afraid to talk about sex. And the Bowling Ball knew how to bust balls, too, especially mine. "You have very small hands," Lil said when I was dating Jeannie and still trying to make a good impression. "Which is perfect, because Jeannie has small boobs." Insulting two people at once, while *possibly* implying they are meant to be together? Italian talent.

This last October was Nani's 99th birthday, impressive to everyone except Nani, with her sights set on 100. She wanted to be 100, and she didn't want to die. Mom says young people assume they'll be ready to die in their eighties or nineties, but that the closer you get to what society deems an "accepted death age," the more afraid you become.

I can't help thinking I'd be okay with it. But by now, everyone else from Nani's lifetime is super dead. Doesn't she want to be with Pop-Pop? Maybe if we told her she was out of money and had to move to Medicare City, she might want to die?

A few months before the 99th, Nani started to trip a bit.

During one hallucination, she snapped at Robyn, "There's broccoli coming in the window."

Robyn didn't miss a beat: "No, there isn't. Listen to yourself; that's crazy talk."

"It is. You're right," Nani laughed, floating down to reality. At that point, Nani had 20/20 vision (with her glasses on) and was still rocking her original teeth, but only had the money for 14 more months of this life.

"What am I gonna do?" Mom would ask, never expecting an answer. "What do we do when she's out of money? Anywhere that accepts Medicare has god-awful reviews. We shouldn't even be moving her at this age. Do I move her in with me and price out in-home care? She keeps saying she wants to live to 100." Her rants started becoming sing-songy. That's when I heard you in my head, clear and as dry as gin.

"So, tell her she's 100," I said.

"What?"

"In October, instead of 99, just tell her she's 100." Dad, you had the thought; I'm just the one who said it out loud. You, still the fixer. Me, the puppet.

And that family of yours, they listened to us. October 16th rolled around, and the stage was set:

- A "Happy 100th Birthday" crown (can't imagine *those* are big sellers).
- "100" iced on cake.
- Great grandkids holding homemade posters with rain-bow-colored 100s drawn haphazardly.
- Her son coming down from Long Island.
- Those who couldn't be there (like me) sending videos pro-claiming the achievement.

That day, Nani Little was lucid, happy, and 100. Three weeks later, she was gone. Now we can rest our wide, flat feet on the coffee table in satisfaction of a job well done, and in your case, to relieve your gout.

Oh shit, she's here? And we didn't *kill her*, you mamaluke, but still … good work. I always knew that bowling ball-shaped grandmother of yours would outlive me. I said it for years, and you all thought I was joking.

"Who am I?" I'd ask, imitating her hunched over: hands on a walker, slowly shuffling, stopping to give a slight lean to the

right, looking down with a minor snort of acknowledgment, then slowly shuffling on by.

Before anyone could say a word, you'd answer yourself: "I'm your grandmother, walking past my open casket 'cause that bitch will never die."

Maybe I didn't end up using a casket. I prefer my coffee can, but I was right that the Bowling Ball outlived me.

The decline was fast—natural causes. Those last few days, Mom stayed in Room 214 around the clock, scared to leave her mother alone in case "it" happened. Robyn and Bryan were visiting and worrying about Mom, who wasn't eating or sleeping much. On one fairly final visit, Robyn brought a bag of popcorn, impulsively thrown in her purse on the way out the door, hoping to get Mom to eat *something*. We can learn a lot from death. One thing is that popcorn is not the ideal snack when sitting with the dying. Popcorn is awkward enough when watching *Terms of Endearment* or *Steel Magnolias*, and really inappropriate during the live show.

Robyn says it took a couple of beats before they realized they were standing over Nani's bed, shoulder to shoulder, eating popcorn while watching *The End*. Robyn and Mom's eyes locked as they slowly maneuvered to face the window, turning their backs on our dying loved one in favor of a salty snack, laughing through tears.

She passed on November 7th. Hospice told us it was "a good one," but we have no reference. There was a funeral at a Catholic church, but I won't bore you with "that voodoo shit." We drove in a procession to her burial plot next to Pop-Pop, purchased decades earlier, down the hill from the rest of the Italians. Once Nani was lowered down, Mom walked her grandchildren up to see the graves of their great-great-grandparents. Right as Bryan's youngest pointed to a family stone, asking, "And who's that?" Mom's drawing of the family tree with her Italian talking hands was interrupted by the funeral director.

"Excuse me, ma'am, but we are only permitted at the gravesite for 30 minutes. We're going over that time, and they will charge you another $200." Grieving is expensive.

We drank sweet Rob Roys at the Afterlife After Party because they were Nani's favorite. It tasted like black licorice doused in hairspray on fire with a cherry. Mom had three and was bombed.

The next week, we cleaned out Nani's room. I took her hairdryer, emery boards, and nail buffer. All items I can picture on her vanity, in that pale pink tiled bathroom, with silver and pink paisley wallpaper, half a wall all mirrored for makeup gazing, and that pink toilet with a soft cushion seat (no cold Italian asses in that house), up on the second floor of her split-level on Roxton Road. I'd play with her glass perfume bottles, pretending to squeeze the long tassels, as she touched up her nose with a power puff and recited her favorite reminder:

"You all wouldn't be here if it weren't for me." We also wouldn't look as good.

In her nineties, when people asked her how she could look so young, she always answered: "Olive oil!" with a fist up in the air. But I knew it was really Oil of Olay moisturizer.

That woman despised me in her younger years, but forgot to hate me towards the end. She had to; I drove her everywhere. The most exercise I got in retirement was getting her in the car. Not *helping her in*, but following behind her walker-shuffle and pretending to kick her ass with my loafers as she was leaving. We both gambled, so once casinos opened in Pennsylvania, she accompanied me. I'd be on the Blackjack tables, your Nan on the slots. I wouldn't say she was lovey-dovey, but we found our rhythm. The sun shines on every dog's ass, eventually.

I choose to think that if we killed your grandmother at 99, it's because she was ready to go. Her life ended up on time. After three generations, people are forgotten anyway. I was ready to

leave the world back when Tom Petty died, three years younger than I was at the time.

Your grandmother was the last person I saw before I died. She had been staying in Long Island, visiting her son Bob with those true 100% Italian grandkids. Not like you half bastards, your mother and I made. Bob and I always split the drive to hand off the Bowling Ball, meeting halfway on the Jersey Turnpike, Exit 8A. I met them that day to bring Lil back to The Home. She'll later tell your mother I wasn't myself, quieter than normal. You're probably thinking we didn't talk on all those drives, but we had some heart-to-hearts.

One time she asked, "Buddy, what is wrong with Jeannie's neck? Do you see that, all that flimsy skin? It's not supposed to look like that."

"It's because she's not fat like us, Lil." See? We got into the thick of it.

Before dropping her at The Home, we stopped for milk at that Royal Farms convenience store where everyone walks out smelling like goddamn fried chicken. She wanted bananas, too, but they were all green.

"We can't afford to buy green bananas at our age," I told her. *Ball-busting is love.* If I'm not busting your balls, *then* you should be worried.

Dad, no one says ball-busting anymore. Can we call it lightly roasting people?

Sure, call me a roastmaster like Dean Martin instead of a ball-buster. It's all the same. So, I brought her up to her apartment, dropped her stuff, and that was it. Me, the Chubb Rock, she, the Bowling Ball, quite a pair. If I'd known that would be the last time I saw her, I would have told her that Bryan shit all over her white couch when he was a baby. But you can't always have that cathartic closure.

Anyway, the back half of life sucks. Sad when Tom Petty died, but I said I wanted the same—quick. Rumor is Petty's final words were: "Do me a favor; never put me in a box." Same. I feel lucky I died still able to wipe my own ass.

Oh, thank God no one but your own mother ever had to wipe your flat, couldn't-hold-up-your-dungarees-so-you-need-suspenders ass. Thanks for that perspective. I shiver to picture it—shit, I just kicked over the *Ballet Slippers* bottle trying to reach my pinky toe with the brush. Now I have a gooey pink bathroom tile situation. Nail polish remover on toilet paper might not cut it.

6

"You can get anything you want at Alice's Restaurant, excepting Alice."

—Arlo Guthrie

It's the Saturday after Thanksgiving, and Mom's here. She started coming to California for the holiday, new traditions, and all. We assemble our "faker" Christmas tree, as Elvis' "Blue Christmas" plays in the background. Over 50 years old and still the #1 selling holiday album of all time. Mom climbs the stepladder to position our giant metal crab as the "star" on top. You were our Christmas Crab.

Everyone who experiences loss says the holidays are the toughest. No revelation there. But I'm surprised this held true for our family because you despised *almost all* holidays, Christmas the most. Thanksgiving, now that was your day. Thanksgiving is about food, booze, and football (translation: gambling). Other than chicken parm with string beans, the traditional Thanksgiving meal was your favorite. You ordered it year-round if we were at one of those diners where you can get anything you want.

Our house had a timed-to-the-minute Thanksgiving tradition. It started back before music could be streamed on demand, in a pocket at all times. Back when we were dependent on DJs to tell us the song title and artist. Back when we kids lay on wall-to-wall carpeting, heads resting next to boomboxes, blank tape inside and at the ready to record whatever we could grab, sending mental requests to the station to play our latest obsession like Ace of Base or something that better stood the test of time like Nirvana. Hitting the record and play buttons simultaneously to catch the magic of Nirvana's "All Apologies," singing along in all our teenage angst, "All alone is all we all." You stepped over us to get to your couch, a throwaway correction: "It's all in all is all we are."

> *Only knowing you to play classic rock, my choker necklace felt even tighter with teenage dilemma: Does this make Dad more cool or Nirvana less cool?*

This was back when, if a good song was playing as you pulled in the driveway, we watched from the windows while you sat in the car until it finished. Back when, on Thanksgiving Day at exactly noon, we would stop pretending to help Mom prepare a meal for 30 people, me unfolding and wiping down cold metal chairs borrowed from a local church (*what* church lent to us heathens?), you hunched over the kitchen table using the "Rotato" peeler, some made-for-TV kitchen gadget which took off more potato than peel.

At noon, we stopped our laboring and for 18 minutes and 34 seconds, we tuned into Philly's 102.9 WMGK classic rock station, cranking up the volume to hear Arlo Guthrie's ballad "Alice's Restaurant Massacree." Tradition, tradition! How did Arlo, son of Woody, remember all those words to his almost 20-minute song built of rapid lyrics that rarely rhyme? You loved a ditty that told a story, and Arlo sure did, recounting how the narrator avoided the draft because of an arrest for illegally dumping trash on Thanksgiving.

In the narrator's defense, there was *already* a pile of trash in that spot on the side of the road. And we all agree, one big pile *is* better than two little piles. "Alice's" is so absurd it must be true. We still play "Alice's" every year, but streaming it without the anticipation, without the risk that we could miss it, without you yelling at us to "Shut up and listen," it's just not the same.

> **Great tune. There we were, listening to a Vietnam protest song well into the '90s. I'm glad I was around when we waited for "Alice's Restaurant" to come on the radio. Saw Arlo do it live once. He could still rock, didn't miss a lick. He's the same age, born in '47.**

> **And my favorite holiday wasn't Thanksgiving, it was March Madness. New Year's Eve got good in the end, too. It's a shitty holiday from about age 14 to 45. First, you want to party when you can't, then when you can, it's never as good as you think. Somewhere in my sixties, we started celebrating with the neighborhood. It was BYOBooze and BYOChristmasLeftovers. We wore our bathrobes, or at least I did. And I could go upstairs to bed any time I wanted. And I did.**

You'd go upstairs for March Madness, too, call your bookie from the bathroom attached to the back bedroom, where voices didn't travel through the floor vents or paper walls. Mom once called me from that upstairs back bathroom—a dual-functioning phone booth—on a favorite holiday of mine: April Fools'.

Unlike you, I love a good prank—when done to others, of course. It's hard to keep a straight face, so my go-to Fools take the form of letters or emails, somewhere I don't have to be present for the big reveal and run the risk of ruining my prank when the corners of my mouth go up involuntarily.

They've often backfired, but I persist. Maybe the worst, most unpredictable reaction was yours in 2007.

I was in law school learning about copyright law while you were following Bob Seger's tour, hitting as many East Coast stadiums as financially possible. You would call us all from the concerts, holding up your flip phone, believing we could hear the music. Stadium sound did not travel well over flip phones. We could barely make out music, let alone the specific song you had determined was personally meant for each one of us. The Philly concert was back in January before the Spectrum was demolished, but you had been making these concert calls for a few months when April Fools' rolled around.

Diligent law student that I was, I fashioned Capitol Records letterhead, complete with the building and stars logo (Seger's label), and mailed you a cease and desist for the illegal and unlicensed reproduction and performance of a Bob Seger concert. It was printed on thick stationery (thank you, Staples) and signed by whoever the internet claimed was the division head. And then I waited.

Instead of a call from you acknowledging my creativity (*I was caught!*) or maybe a rant (*is this real?*) about how there is no more art in this world, only business, Mom called me at school on my own flip phone.

"Jenny, I'm upstairs in the back bathroom. Can you hear me?"

"Yeah, what's wrong?"

"Well …" Long pause. "Dad got the letter."

"Is he so mad?"

"It's much worse. He thinks the letter is real, and he loves it. He's calling all his friends. He wants to frame it."

"Oh, fuck." *Once you put art out there, you can't control how it's received.*

See, another holiday ruined. I don't even remember that, and I don't remember many good Christmases, either. Maybe that time in March when I accidentally wore a Christmas tie to the office? Borrowed it from your brother's closet. Better than a tie clip, it had a clever round weight in the bottom, so the tie didn't swing around my gut.

First meeting of the day, someone reached over, grabbed my tie, pressed the weight, and Christmas music seeped through. Word got around, and I couldn't close my office door. All day long, everyone coming in to play that damn tie. Now remember, this was a Jewish district, and I was one of the few Gentiles working there. Jewish people love Christmas music. Hell, they wrote most of it, all the good ones anyway.

So, you admit, there are good Christmas songs? Christmas has its own soundtrack. It's not a holiday; it's a *season*. Now, Christmas starts the day after Halloween, usurps Thanksgiving, and drags its festive balls all the way to New Year's. The sheer duration of this calendared forced fun made it the hardest when we lost you, our fat and (mostly) jolly Father Christmas.

We rejoiced in your hatred of Christmas. You kept us guessing which events you would hate more:

Crowded Standing-Room-Only Christmas Eve Mass

vs.

Public School Children's Holiday Concert Singing Off-Key Unknown Secular Songs

Or which decoration would irritate you most:

Electric Candles That Burned Festive Red Circles Into Your Plastic Blinds

vs.

Crooked Christmas Tree Anchored to the Wall with Fishing Wire

Every comedian needs his straight man, and Mom was the Dean Martin to your Jerry Lewis. She positioned holiday decorations approximately six inches apart on every flat surface throughout the house. You claimed these knick-knacks were strategically placed so that no coffee mug could be put down during the Christmas season.

She would bake her pizzelles but admonish you that they were *only for guests* and continued to fill our stockings even as we ~~kids~~ entered our forties. And while she did all this, do you remember what you did?

That's right, you simply sat on the couch. As the rest of us decorated the tree, accompanying the 24-hour Christmas music station was your bitching and moaning. Your greatest hits were about the cost and wasted energy of Christmas, but the subject of individual gripes varied.

Potential lyrics of your woulda-been-a-hit Christmas Classic:

"Stop putting the ornaments so damn close."

"We keep those popcorn strings from year to year? That's disgusting."

"That giant bow on top looks god-awful."

"What's wrong with using the ugly-ass angel that the whack-job neighbor made?"

Odd that you, a guy who changed his clothes once a week and owned the same pair of loafers until your gout blew a hole in them, fancied himself an expert interior decorator.

But these *accidental* traditions crept up through the years. While we didn't specifically tune in to hear your rants, they became the soundtrack to our holiday. When Bud bitched, we listened. You were our scotched-up Grinch.

What you call tradition was just our routine. We had one good Christmas routine: watching the cult classic movie *29th Street* every Christmas Eve. Rumored to be about the first winner of the New York State Lottery back in '76, from a family of Italian New Yorkers set at Christmas. One of my favorite lines from the

son talking to his father about his hopes and dreams reminds me of you kids:

Frank Pesce Jr.: "I wanna do something I never did before."

Frank Pesce Sr.: "Oh really, then why don't you go upstairs and clean your fucking room?"

These holidays are all made up, too. If you're so bored with them, then why don't you go clean your fucking room?

But I can't imagine you hated it *all* that much. You acknowledged it enough to invent the game "Bad Santa" for your grandkids. You were an easy target, rarely leaving that red corduroy couch (especially during football/basketball/baseball/golf/hockey-if-you-have-to season). The kids would climb into your lap, pretending you were Santa, knowing full well what you'd do.

They'd plead, "Do Bad Santa."

"And what do *you* want for Christmas, little kid?" you would croon in a voice reserved for wolves dressed as grandmothers.

The moment the kid said whatever popular crap toy they wanted, in that split second (the only time you moved fast), you grabbed the kid's head with your chubby hands, one palming their entire face basketball-style, the other holding the back of the head (safety precaution?), and you shook their little noggin, tipping them upside down, head inches from the floor, while you roared *"YOU GET NOTHING,"* as they squealed in fearful delight.

Clever. But it wasn't lost on me that this holiday game your grandkids worshiped was merely a remake of *Disha Disha*, the game you invented for your own kids. No new material, Bud? There were minor differences.

In *Bad Santa*, the kid's fate was predetermined. They were always going to *GET NOTHING* and get crushed. In your original '80s version, much stranger, we picked our fate. And still, we almost always picked the pants-wetting, face-crushing choice.

We'd saddle up next to you in our OshKosh B'Gosh as you camped out on your couch-throne (back then, like much of the '80s, tweed, plaid, and scratchy). With our kiddie hands barely covering your plump cheeks, you would immediately close your eyes and faintly ask, "What are you doing …?" trailing off, as if being hypnotized. We'd knead your face in a circular motion while chanting (in what we hoped was a mysterious voice) one of two choices:

<u>Option One:</u> *"Disha Disha Daddy **Woo W**oo."*

This chant turned you into a giant walking baby. Eyes still closed, you would not-so-gently pat down our heads, plastering our faces with our long hair (possibly permed, depending on the year), so we couldn't see. All the while making whining noises: "Aw, Daddy Woo Woo." Sure, that was weird fun.

But what did we choose 80% of the time?

<u>Option Two:</u> "Disha Disha Daddy **Goo G**oo."

This chant, one letter off, made you go berserk. You turned on us with the frenzy of *Bad Santa*, only a little rougher since we were your own kids. You palmed our tiny faces with a chubby paw and shook the shit out of us while yelling, "Daddy Goo Goo" in a crazed voice. And if we happened to wiggle away from your grip? Enraged, you'd stomp through the house, Lou-Ferrigno-Incredible-Hulk-style, as we ran in glee, at times peeing a little in those OshKosh.

To turn you back into Dad, one of us needed to boldly approach the monster, rubbing its cheeks and chanting all over again. You'd come to, feigning amnesia, "Wait, where am I? What happened?" We'd topple over in pure kid glee, believing we'd cast a spell on you. We took the gamble and got the thrill. We were magic. You were magic.

We never played board games as a family. We played solitaire and made it interactive by standing over the poor schlub playing and pointing out moves before they saw 'em: "Ten on the Jack." Ruining solitaire for each other and Disha Disha are the only games

I remember, except once when it stormed down the shore and we sat around naming songs with the word "rain" in them.

When people ask me, "Didn't you play Monopoly as a kid?" immediately I think, *Oh no, I played Disha Disha, where I bet my little life. If I picked the safe route, sure, it was silly fun. But when I chose to turn my father into a raging monster? Well, that scared the bejesus out of me, and I lived to tell about it.*

Disha Disha is long gone, but now there's not even Bad Santa. Christmas without you is like *Meet Me in St. Louis*—that Judy Garland movie about a family moving to New York who, in the end, decides not to move: Nothing interesting happens.

> **—Christ Almighty, kid, you sure do overanalyze. Disha Disha was invented to make time pass. Simple parental necessity. And maybe a bit of nostalgia for back when I could legally give you an arm yank with a smack on the bottom when you were goofing off. I hear they frown on that nowadays. I don't know what to tell you about our boring-ass family. Maybe you, yourself, could get more interesting? If I could paraphrase Seger:**
>
> *You want to dream like a young woman with the wisdom of an old woman.*
>
> *But the thing is, you just can't have it all.*

But this boredom is deafening. Mom doesn't send Christmas cards anymore because you were the star of them. How can she compete with the picture of you on the front, dressed in your standard-issue golf windbreaker, next to the neighbor dressed as Santa, where the inside asked: "*Which fat bastard do you dislike more?*" Or the time you were pictured in a Santa hat, hands cradling your bowl-full-of-jelly belly with a look of pain on your face, with the inside: "*Happy Holidays. I'm making a Yule Log just for you!*" She could never rival the time you sat on a toilet (fully clothed, thank God), that was left outside on the front lawn (please tell me you were remodeling?), reading a newspaper with the greeting: "*Happy Holidays. Hope*

You're 'Flush' in the New Year." Dean needs Jerry. Jean needs Buddy.

This boredom is annoying. More annoying than your constant, empty threat at restaurants: "Don't fill up on bread!" Thanksgiving was always gonna be screwed without you. That was your meal. But how our Christmas curmudgeon managed to ruin that entire season for us is mystifying. Dull doesn't come close to describing our holidays now. For me, it's like watching the 24-hour golf channel. For you, it would be like sitting through your child's cavalcade, those marching band competitions without any football game, dubbed the "Halftime from Hell." Sure, there's no more Johnny Walker, but there's also no Bad Santa. Who wants to listen to Dean Martin Christmas carols without any bitching in the background about the money and time being wasted? Nobody wants that sticky-sweet *Marshmallow World*. We need our Grinch.

My hostility toward Christmas wasn't a put-on. It wasn't to entertain you all. There are reasons that I got up from the table every Christmas Eve, walked out the front door, and stood with Bryan's father-in-law, Bernie, to bitch about that fucking holiday out in the bitter cold, where you could have shoved a stick up my ass cause I was a goddamn popsicle, standing with my back to those shitty twinkle lights. And it wasn't only the years when I placed some bad bets. I needed to stand with those lights your mother strung up that were causing my electricity bill to go through the roof, that sonofabitch Santa is supposedly gonna walk on in order to yell about all the crap we bought and how I spent hundreds on dinner for 20 people.

Bitching with Bernie, now there's a tradition for ya. Do you think I took an adjunct professor role every fall for fun? For passion? I already had a full-time job. My holiday hatred runs longer and deeper than my debt.

Growing up, we were piss-poor. Sure, we lived in a good house, on a good street, with a good address, but I'm talking *no dough*. We could occasionally afford Junket, that favorite jelly dessert of

mine, but that's about it. One nun at school tortured us because we had a Drexel Hill address; she thought we had money, but all we had was that address.

One time, your Pop-Pop brought home a pair of hand-me-down black Oxford-looking shoes. The original owner had had polio, so one shoe had an extra three-inch Herman Munster heel to compensate for a limp. I can't remember which one of us four boys had to wear 'em. Like my mother's favorite Christmas song:

I am a poor boy, too, pa rum bu bu bum.

I have no gift to bring, pa rum bu bu bum.

My father spent our Christmas Eves tying one on at the Legion. Then he carried home the saddest piece of shit Charlie Brown Christmas tree you ever saw. He hated that holiday for sure and spent it in the cups. But he also became a Pop-Pop who went down to the basement on Christmas Eve and called "Ho, ho, ho" right up the chimney. Got your brother so excited, the kid did a flip in the air.

I do recall money well spent one Christmas. Somewhere in the '90s, when we were Chreasters (Christians only on Christmas & Easter), we got to St. Mary's early enough to get seats for mass. I was next to my brother Bob, and as the collection basket started coming around, your mother, sitting in the row behind us, reached over my shoulder and handed me $20. If there is a God, he spoke to me in that moment as the organist started the offertory hymn "Be Not Afraid."

"Watch this," I told Bob. I reached into my pocket and removed $1 from my rubber-banded wad of cash, then folded the $20 in front of the $1 so that the big bill showed. When the collection basket came around, it was one of those with the long handles where the usher was holding on, watching each drop. My fat fingers moved faster than changing channels on the remote as I flipped the bills, placing the $1 in the basket and covering the $20 with my chubby palm until I got it safely back into my rubber band.

My brother's shoulders started shaking up and down, up and down, and then the tears started rolling down his face till Jeannie knew something was up. I confessed, so I could forever tell the story of my Christmas Miracle. I put that $20 on football the next day, well, that plus another $80.

All religion was invented by man; it's voodoo. Plus, how come I never saw a Jesus sticker on a Porsche?

Dear Jen & Rusty,

Happy Holidays

I'm making a Yule Log just
for you!

Love
and best wishes
for 2014,
Nora & Buddy Pop

**Please Do Not Feed
Me Any Treats!**
I have to
watch my weight...
Thank You

Happy Holidays
from someone
who's not too "stable"!

HEARTFULLY YOURS
Bud

The burning

yuletide

question...

Which fat bastard do you dislike more?

Make Christmas
Great Again...

Just
grab it!

7

"If only I could have a friend
Who'd stick with me until the end."

—Harry Nilsson

As I try to type, Stevie Licks pushes my elbow up with her big snotty nose, telling me it's time for a walk. I've never had an 80-lb. dog before, and this one uses all those pounds to tell me what to do. Must be the cattle dog in her. I grab her leash, throw on a jacket, and put on a playlist I made for you years ago: Chuck's Licks.

For the first couple of years right after you died, I couldn't listen to classic rock. If one of "your songs" came on the radio, my arm shot out, changing the station by the third note. When it came to Bob Seger, I was quick enough to change on the first note. You only left me with The Beatles, which wasn't so bad. That gave me 12 studio albums, 5 live albums, 49 compilations, 36 Eps, and 37 box sets to choose from. You had a healthy respect for the Fab Four, but somehow Beatle Mania never afflicted you.

I'm not saying you would change the station when they came on, but we never went searching for them. You had some Beatles opinions that I took as gospel.

"You know," you'd lecture to any car-captive audience who happened to ride with you on Sunday mornings when 102.9 WMGK played its two-hour *Breakfast with The Beatles* program, "the best Beatles song was *Here Comes the Sun*, and George Harrison wrote it. He shoulda written more for them, but he couldn't get out from behind John and Paul." I still take these gems as fact. But then, even at 20, I was pretty sure your sweeping dismissal of Yoko Ono was both sexist and misinformed.

> I said it then, and I'll say it again. I told you when I picked you up for spring break, and we drove to the Rock & Roll Hall of Fame in Cleveland. The fourth floor was entirely dedicated to The Beatles. An old black rotary phone sat on a table in the corner, and only Yoko had the number. She could call it, and anyone standing around could pick it up. "Why in the hell would I wanna talk to her?" I made sure the whole floor heard me.

> You know, I never saw Roy Orbison live, but I saw his horn-rimmed glasses next to his black guitar on a wall. They didn't let you take pictures, and I wouldn't have had a camera anyway, but that was a fine memory.

> I tried to teach you more on that trip than you were ready for. Our hotel had a free happy hour every night from five to seven. I would sit you at a table toward the back and go up to the bar for both of us. First, you asked for a screwdriver. Then a Kahlúa and cream. Then a White Russian, which is the same goddamn thing, no? Finally, you asked for some kind of a breezy vodka drink. No.

> "You pick one drink, and you drink it all night. Never mix drinks, or you'll get sick." I cut you off without giving you the tip that you can always end with a beer.

I went to a Rock & Roll Hall of Fame Induction Ceremony a few years ago. You and I talked about going to this ultimate concert together, but we never quite planned the trip. Once I heard Dolly Parton was getting inducted, I made it happen. You would have loved the inductees. I will lay them out in order of *your* increasing adoration: Pat Benatar and Neil Giraldo, Eurythmics, Lionel Richie,

Dolly Parton, and Carly Simon. But it wasn't only the inductees, it was the *"Anticipation, anticipation … keepin' me waiting,"* as Carly sang for the presenters and other performers to appear on stage. The audience knew who was getting inducted, but we didn't know who else was gonna show up.

For six hours, it was one, as you would proclaim, "Knock-your-socks-off" appearance after another. I was high on suspense and the nose-bleeding altitude of our last-row seats. Mellencamp, Alice Cooper, Steven Tyler, The Edge, the Boss, that kid Ed Sheeran that you liked—all performed. Mellencamp and Springsteen sang *Great Balls Of Fire*, a tribute to Jerry Lee Lewis, another inaugural inductee.

> **You know, Jerry Lee married his cousin when she was 13. The guy had seven wives total, which is batshit anyway. But it was the cousin thing that he *never* lived down.**

Well, it didn't come up at the ceremony. Mellencamp came out and inducted his legal counsel, Allen Grubman, the first lawyer in the Rock & Roll Hall of Fame. I whooped as loudly for Allen as for Dolly. This guy represented *everyone*: Springsteen, U2, Madonna, Elton, Gaga, even singers with more than one name. He changed the entire business, fighting for artists to keep creative control of their work. Bonus, he looks exactly like what anyone wants their lawyer to look like: round-ish, Jewish, New York-ish, with a full head of salt (no more pepper) hair, and smiley eyes for having a beer with. He cried when they inducted him.

Besides The Beatles, you left us with your dog, Sophie. Her full name was Sophie the Dog, like Alexander the Great. Had to have the "the," like The Beatles. Not sure if you would cop to this now, but let the record show: You did not want Sophie the Dog.

> **Dogs die; it's too painful. I hated cats, and I couldn't even stand to have one of those die. You know, I told everyone I couldn't be around cats because of my allergies. If I were going to someone's**

house, I asked if the cat could be put in a room, told 'em it was so I could breathe. That wasn't it. When I was little, I watched my older brother Bob get attacked by a cat. That was enough to scare the shit out of me for a lifetime.

We got a puppy cockapoo from Diane's Discount Pets right down Rte. 100. Sophie the Dog was so young, she fit in cupped hands—beige curls on top of beige curls; she had the opposite coloring from our first dog, Emma, on purpose. This was the year you retired and were home all day with this "not-yet-your" dog. Our couch at the time was beige with a brown cattail reed design. Surprising that someone saw cattails in a marsh and thought: *Let's put that on a sofa!* Sophie the Dog had a habit of burrowing into this couch and sticking her little brown nose out from between the cushions to breathe. I was always scared you'd grab the remote, turn on the TV, plop down, and crush her.

Instead, she became your curly, stocky shadow. The two of you were back and forth to the fridge all day, hoping to find something new in there. She enjoyed the same deli meats, cheese blocks, and pepperoni—really, anything that came out of your shared lunch meat drawer. She kept the same odd hours: up until midnight, with an afternoon nap or two.

When she was too old to jump on the bed, her back legs giving out, Mom bought her stairs she never used. Instead, you bent over, releasing a deep, guttural sound to pick her up. With your bad heart, the pair of you with your stumpy legs, simply walked across Styer Road and back each day, 492 feet one way.

Courtesy of you, Sophie only knew one game. Rules & Instructions for Sophie's One and Only Game:

1. The Human sits down, could be on the cattail sofa, but any seat will do.
2. The Human extends one leg straight, flexed ankle resting on the floor.

3. Sophie the Dog retrieves a squeaky toy.
4. With said toy in mouth, she rests the toy on the Human's shin.
5. The Human moves said leg up and down, like lifting the needle on a record player.
6. The Human's gaze can remain on the television.
7. Sophie the Dog squeaks the moving toy, happily occupied.

And if she wasn't playing her one game, she was napping at your feet as you flipped through the channels. Your Sophie the Dog seesaw game always makes me sing-say that nursery rhyme we learned as kids:

Seesaw, knock at the door.
Who's there?
Grandpa.
Whaddaya want?
A glass of beer.
Where's your money?
In my pocket.
Where's your pocket?
In my pants.
Where's your pants?
I left 'em home.
GET OUTTA HERE, YA DRUNKIN' BUM!

I have some questions about our nursery rhythms and Grandpa's lack of pants, but I'll save those for later. For now, that is the laziest game a dog ever played. But then that puppy was retired, just like you.

Speaking of lazy, what about you slobs who got up from the kitchen table, leaving your chair out? How many times did I hafta yell, "Push your chair in!" while Sophie the Dog jumped from your chair onto the table to eat the rest of a meal? That's your fault, not hers. Clean plate club.

She *never* got reprimanded; it was always our fault. She didn't even have to learn any tricks. Was never asked to sit, fetch, roll over, or play dead.

> **Why does the dog have to sit on command? It's her life. Plus, she was close enough to the floor as it was; sitting couldn't get her any closer. She barked and carried on when folks came to the door, but I didn't mind. I'd tell them: "*She'll just lick you to death.*" She was a good dog.**

You *always* took the dog's side. What about the time my dog bit you across the nose? You and Mom were watching my half-a-beagle, Cracklin' Rosie, while Rusty and I were away. Your boarding facilities were a pretty good deal: free. As you told the story, Rosie was curled up with Mom on the couch. You wanted your neck rubbed, so you (stupidly) plopped down on the floor in front, where Mom sat. I can't imagine you moved fast, so it must have been a hard sit. Rosie jumped to Mom's defense, flew through the air, and bit you on the nose. I saw the boxer-like scar when I picked her up. You maintained that you "had it coming." The animal was always right.

Sophie had some health issues, but as the favorite child, she was constantly monitored. It took a while and hundreds in vet bills to find out she was allergic to chicken—had to be a reason for all that scratching. Eventually, it was determined that she had Cushing's disease. This meant that you were a regular at the Ludwig's Corner Vet. You probably ran a tab there, like it was a tavern. Too many parallels are drawn between people and their pets, but when I look at the symptoms of Cushing's, I can't help but wonder: Did you both have it?

Cushing's Symptoms	Sophie (aka Sophie The Dog, Sopha-Lofa)	Dad (aka Bud, Uncle Budget, Chubb Rock)
Increased thirst	Water bowls placed strategically throughout the house (and periodically tripped on by humans).	See Chapter 9.
Increased urination	Constant opening of back door for "peepees outside."	On Lasix, likely peed outside at a golf course or two.
Increased appetite	Snausages.	Sausages.
Reduced activity	*See < 1,000-foot walk above.	Rented a cart to golf.
Hair loss	Once curly blonde fur turned into wispy down feathers.	Top gone, let it grow down the sides, called it your "Bernie Madoff."
Recurrent skin infections	Skin tags everywhere.	Skin tags everywhere, called them "hanging chads."

Sophie lived a good life, especially when we didn't push in our chairs. All that people food, no real exercise, and your dog lived to be 17. By that age, Mom was holding her together with duct tape. (*I wish I were joking.*) She put stickers on the bottom of Sophie's paws to give her traction as her short little legs would slide out from under her. Sophie was semi-blind, and the bright sun bothered her. So, when she went outside, with her sticker paws, she wore tinted goggles. By this point, she had gone deaf in her big floppy ears, so good luck calling her to come back inside. But goddamnit if Mom wasn't gonna keep her alive.

Harrison also wrote "All Things Must Pass" the same year your mother and I got married. A song of balance, reminding us that "Sunset doesn't last all evening" and that "It's not always going to be this grey."

You were gone three years when Sophie was put down. It was like losing you all over again. I took a red-eye to "be supportive." Since Sophie the Dog was a *big spender* and a VIP, the vet came to the house. We sat in your den. I dropped into a type of fetal position in the big red chair in the opposite corner of the room and didn't move again. Mom sat on the floor, cradling Sophie the Dog, feeding her iced animal crackers, and telling her how she was the bestest, sweetest dog in the whole wide world. I worked to control my breath and keep my sobs silent, but at one point, I let out a gut-wrench of a wail.

Afterward, Robyn made sure to tell me, "Thank god you came home; what would we do without you?" as she impersonated my sobs. Unlike you, Sophie the Dog had many possessions. I inherited one of Sophie's toys, a teal stuffed bone (squeaker still intact) with "I'm kind of a big deal" embroidered on it. It should also say, "So, push in your chair."

Sophie and I were meant to be. The Beatles had a song, "Martha My Dear," that Paul always said was about his sheepdog. When he sang about that "silly girl," I think he was singing about Sophie the Dog:

> *When you find yourself in the thick of it*
>
> *Help yourself to a bit of what is all around you ...*

Sophie sure did that.

Slowly, classic rock stopped making me cry. Or it started to feel good to cry, and I went radio-diving for it, or I'll put on Chuck's Licks when I'm out for a walk with Stevie Licks (named after Stevie Nicks, not your playlist). As I walk Stevie along the coastal trail by our house, I'll sit on one of the memorial benches; they are all dedicated to someone. The one closest to our house says:

"Never Miss a Sunset." –AA

Not sure who AA is, but I agree. I've thought about dedicating a bench to you.

"For Bud, who would never walk this far."

Eventually, the songs started to feel like you were a hitchhiker in my car, or sitting on the bench with me and Stevie. When "Against the Wind's" first few bars of G come on, if Rusty reaches out to change the station for me, I admonish him: "Whoa, I don't hang up on your dad when he calls." But it's still nice to have The Beatles in case I want to drive alone.

8

"Put your makeup on, fix your hair up pretty, And **meet me tonight in Atlantic City."**

—Bruce Springsteen

During her summer break, Robyn flew in to see our new house for the first time. As she walked around, I wondered if she noticed I didn't have any pictures of you. I don't hang photos; I hate the way they show the passage of time.

Robyn, on the other hand, strategically places 4x6 framed pictures of you throughout her house. Sometimes she adds new "old" ones to her fridge, reminding her kids of their Buddy Pop.

Bryan built you a shrine—a series of framed classic rock album covers lining his basement stairs, ending on the last step in a big picture of you. It warms my heart to think of how much all of this would disgust you.

We drove up to Lake Tahoe for the weekend, Robyn bracing with each twist up the mountain, pointing out every spot without a guardrail. She clutched the "Oh, Shit!" handle with both hands as we took the road between Cascade Lake and Emerald Bay, a sheer drop off each side into Bombay Sapphire blue water. The same spot where you held onto that same handle seven years earlier, telling me your butt cheeks had never clenched so tight.

"Dad came here and could barely breathe with the altitude. I dropped him at the casino for the day," I said, trying to take her mind off the cliffs.

—And it snowed a foot overnight. What a trip. It was so cold, you could kick a dog turd. But worse than asphyxiation and frostbite, you took me there on Thanksgiving and rented a house *without* cable. No cable on the biggest football weekend of the year. I had hundreds on the games. Nothing I could do but sit and wait, and call my bookie from the commode.

"I want to gamble!" Robyn immediately altered our mountain air trip. "Take me to the one he went to. Silly, but makes me feel close to him." She always says what she feels at the exact moment she feels it; it's unnerving.

I found a vista point to turn us around, winding back down the mountain, away from the calming pines and toward the casino towers with their neon lights misplaced against nature. As I pulled into the crowded parking lot, full of tour buses and RVs, it was nothing like Simon & Garfunkel's calming "The Sound of Silence," except that everyone came *to bow and pray to the neon god they made*: gambling machines.

The casino, the biggest in Tahoe, felt like a once-famous rocker— vocal cords atrophied—who'd had a rough life on the road. Bubble gum music played, meant to keep us there, but the smoke that slapped me across the face as we entered made me want to run. It was 4:00 p.m. on a Monday, but there weren't many tables open. The open ones were $25 buy-ins, and all of a sudden, through the smoke, dim music, and dim lighting, I was transported back with you, *Old Friend*, on our first casino trip.

I must have been home from college for Thanksgiving. The whole family went to Boardwalk Hall to see Simon & Garfunkel's 2003

"Old Friends" reunion tour. Great seats. I cried when they sang "Kathy's Song." It was so damn beautiful. I remember thinking in the dramatic, absurd mind of a twenty-something: *Maybe I should never see another concert ever again, make this my last.* Ridiculous thou—

Might as well. They don't make good music anyway these days.

Hold the bitching and moaning for a minute, would ya? I'm remembering my old man. Now, if anything hanging in my house reminds me of you, it's the framed black and white poster from that concert. The title "Old Friends" is in quotations, as if a pun on their lack of friendship instead of the title of their song and the name of the tour itself.

You bought me the poster as we left the show, walking out onto the boardwalk night. But do you remember how I got the poster *framed*? College kids can't afford to custom-frame a concert poster. No, they need that money for booze. In college, you have barely enough in the bank to go to the concert, and if you can buy the poster, you hang it up with Scotch Tape that eventually pulls the white paint from your rented walls.

But my poster is framed, *with the ticket cut out of the matting*, and when I look at it, I don't wonder if Tom & Jerry (as originally known) are truly *Old Friends* or if they're no longer speaking. I think of you. I hear painfully perfect music, and I wonder about how high your gambling stakes were.

Did you go to hear "I Am a Rock," or did you go to gamble in AC? Little of Column A, little of Column B? After the show, all five of us stayed overnight, sharing one casino hotel room because:

5 people x $125 per ticket = A lotta dough

You covered the room and all our meals with those magical casino vouchers. We knew not to ask how you earned them. I had just turned 21, and after the show, you took me to the Tropicana to teach me Blackjack. No one else came with us; they went right to sleep. Were they tired from the concert? Or did they know then what I'm not even sure about now?

> *Bryan's never been much of a gambler. Robyn loves it;*
> *she's got the itch, but not the full rash.*

This is why she'll spend an afternoon in a Tahoe casino, worlds away from the pristine blue lake across the street. She saddled up to video Blackjack, yelling "Pay the lady," as she got her $40 up to $90, ordered a drink, and informed me we're staying for more. She eventually walked away up $10. She takes her Kenny Rogers seriously: knows when to fold 'em.

Why does she play those crap machines with the bullshit lights and all that buzzing? That's not the game. The game has a real-life dealer, human players, wet drinks, and tips. It's not as social as golf; it's social without being social. You gotta see the dealer's face, the other players' reactions, the cards they're showing. You can place a side bet for the dealer, get 'em on your side. Make some good juju for yourself. The odds might be in the house's favor, but only slightly. You can't feel those chances on a machine.

As kids, while others played Nintendo, we played a handheld electronic Blackjack game someone had given you as a gift. With Blackjack, did you need a poker face? If you were good at bluffing, I have to tell you, none of us inherited that. Every time Bryan lies, the corners of his mouth curl up. Robyn is honest to a fault; she'll give you the plans to the missile base. Even me, the one whose job is one big negotiation, I can't stand the posturing. What a waste of time.

Robyn is only five years older than me, but she not only recognized all your gambling habits, she loves to play. As I watched her command the video Poker machine, she explained her moves: "Dad always said hitting on 12 depends on how many cards the dealer has. See, here he would tell me to split." When did you say all this? Where was I? I am jealous of her memories.

Robyn was your companion-accomplice too many times. Twenty years ago, at that concert, she knew that while the highs were high, the lows could mean being asked to take out a cash advance on her credit card. She'll tell me there were times you didn't have the toll for the Jersey Turnpike, that you invited your bookie to her wedding, that her bedroom was next to yours and she heard Mom crying when you were thousands "in the hole" (as you put it) in AC.

Robyn had your number. She was the one who told me that you were always in that upstairs bathroom, making calls on the cordless to your bookie. I'd sneak into your bedroom to listen, but you sounded like small potatoes: "Put a dollar on Dallas." *He's only betting a dollar? Why is Mom annoyed? Is it because he's betting against the Eagles?* I'm embarrassed to say how long it was before I learned that "a dollar" was $100. Of course, Mom knew the most. She knew that when you were at the table, you couldn't see, couldn't hear, you weren't even really there. I wish I didn't know now what I didn't know then.

I *was* small potatoes. Your sister? She's not even a spud. Lots of people take out second mortgages; I didn't do that 'cause I put the first one down at the tables. If you add it all up, we're talking cars, not homes. Did I gamble? Yes. Did I gamble too much? Depends who you ask. Did I come home for dinner every night and take out loans to help put you all through school? Sure did.

I wasn't the Tuesday afternoon gambler or the Friday paycheck gambler. Atlantic City was two hours from the house. If I wanted, I coulda been there every weekend. Back in 2010, they opened casinos in Philly. I could have been there *daily*, but I wasn't.

Maybe it was restraint, or maybe it was because Philly started out with shitty slots.

And I didn't *always* hide in the upstairs bathroom to call my bookie. Once I started teaching at that Catholic university, I had an office for calling in my bets. Of course, I shared that office

with Sister Mary Chapman. Remember, without Mrs. Hermann, I was lost.

Sister Mary taught me how to type a capital letter on the computer. If only one of us can get into heaven, it really should be Sister Mary. To keep her salvation safe, each time I opened my flip phone to place a wager, I warned her: "Don't listen." Like nose picking in the car, I guess I was always trying not to get caught.

And didn't you gamble thousands on that classic car you can't even drive? From where I'm sitting, that's a bad hand. My winnings can *make more* winnings. Your "winnings" just leak oil.

Back at the Tropicana, you knew how to read the floor that night. When the automatic doors swung open, I hacked as that wall of smoke hit us. You sped past tables in your Docksiders and dungarees. Hands in both pockets, making those 32" length pants even shorter. I skipped to keep up, oozing maturity with my ponytail extra high and tight, balancing the rolled-up Simon & Garfunkel poster under my arm.

But remember, this was Saturday night in America's Playground. We searched for a $5 table, heck, even a $10 table—nothing. "Screw it," you said as we sat down at a $25 buy-in. And then everything began to move at the unspoken speed of gamblers. By the time I added up my two cards, you had already made the stay/hit/split decision for both our hands, and the dealer had moved down the table. I was holding up the game—your game. My heart was racing, and all I wanted was what every college kid wants: a free drink. Before the waitress came back with my White Russian, we were down $900. To me, $900 was the cost of my car. My rent was $325 a month. I started ever so slightly swiveling in my armless casino chair.

You turned and simply said, "Go to bed. I'll get it back." And I did. And you did. You came into the room, maybe at 5:00 a.m., when all of us were asleep. I learned you had won it all back *and then some.*

Something in the four digits for sure. You handed me a $100 bill, and I used it to frame the poster with my ticket.

That was the first time I saw that you had no hope and no patience. The highs are high, but you gotta learn to wait out a loss 'cause they're inevitable. The minute we were down, you looked like you shit your pants, and it wasn't even your money.

The next time I saw that face was when I took you to purchase lotto tickets. It was back when the new Powerball multi-state lotto came out. Odds were worse, but the jackpot was bigger. No one had won yet, and the pot was Meatloaf-sized.

We headed to Top of the Hill Beverage, that drive-through liquor store for the real drinkers who don't need to get out of the car; they know what they want. I asked for $20 worth of tickets, and as I leaned toward the drive-up window, you casually asked me to get you a couple of tickets for your boyfriend at the time.

I couldn't have looked at you with more disdain if I'd tried.

"I'll pay for it." You tried handing me $5 in protest, your face uneasy and confused, like sitting down on a toilet seat that's still warm from the last person.

I still can't believe a kid of mine thought a lotto ticket was an appropriate gift.

"What if he actually *wins?*" I bellowed. "What would you do *then?* You would give someone *millions* of dollars?" You smiled as if that would be a good turn of events. "I'll get you a ticket if you promise not to give it away."

"Nah, that's okay." Idiot kid of mine didn't have the hope.

We spent the rest of the car ride listing out the pros and cons of getting the winnings in one large lump sum or paid out over time. An annuity payment is more in the end, plus it means you can't go nuts. But the lump sum means you can take care of taxes off the bat, invest it, and you don't have someone else holding onto your money. Plus, you might not live long enough to get all that annuity. I chose lump sum. You chose annuity.

You know, you lose 100% of the lotteries you don't buy a ticket for. Wayne Gretzky mighta said that.

The concert ticket is old and faded, which I guess is what happens with *Old Friends*. And I know you touched this ticket because you picked them up for us at Will Call. Section 121, on the end. Always have an aisle seat for dancing. This is true even for your particular, understated dance move: eyes scrunched up, biting lower lip, fist out at a 45-degree angle, keeping the beat with a hammer motion, knees slightly bent to allow a small bounce. Gotta have an aisle seat for those moves. And I hate to break it to you, but Dad, they don't make paper tickets anymore.

9

"*When I drink alone,*
I prefer to be by myself."

—George Thorogood

We had a global pandemic. At first, they called the virus Corona, like the beer. But then they rebranded it to COVID-19. Maybe the beer lobbyists got to them.

Millions died. Funerals had attendance limits; some were online. It would be hard to attend a funeral online and not bring a comforting cup of coffee to the screen as a refreshment. My friend Elizabeth's husband died—cancer, not COVID. The funeral was limited to 20 people. My Irish Catholic redheaded friend explained that since her husband came from an Indian family, this wouldn't even cover his siblings and their children.

A few weeks after his mostly online funeral, I asked her to go on a hike along the coast. "Hike" is how we Californians say, "walk outside" to impress. It was particularly hard to come up with pandemic-approved socializing with a grieving spouse. After this COVID-sanctioned outdoor activity, Elizabeth surprised me by saying, "I could go for a drink." It was five o'clock somewhere …

The closest bar happened to also be the *saltiest* bar in town. The one that bucked pandemic protocols and stayed open during lockdown. Town rumor was that the cops didn't want to close down their own watering hole.

We pushed open the door, wearing hiking boots and backpacks. Elizabeth carried walking poles, gear that suggested Yosemite, not the paved coastal path we had just "hiked." Old and sticky whiffs of dried beer and pretzel salt hit our nostrils as our eyes adjusted to almost utter darkness, except for the neon beer signs and TVs behind the bar playing sports, sports, and more sports. Sports memorabilia covered the walls, and retired surfboards hung from the rafters. Peanut shells on the floor would have improved the place.

Neither of us had been to a bar since the pandemic started. Every business had different rules for social distancing: single-file, three lines, not one; order food and drinks separately; scan a QR code; order online, and pick up at a window. We immediately linked arms.

"How do you order here?" Elizabeth asked.

"No clue. Where's the line?" I scanned the barflies with their butts in seats, chins up, eyes glued to a 49ers game. No one noticed us. The barback coughed as he rinsed glasses, or maybe he cleared his throat.

"Do you think we go up to the bar?"

She shrugged.

Arms still locked, we performed a three-legged-race-style walk toward the bar, as uncomfortable as minors using fake IDs. *How did I forget how to order at a bar?*

I scanned the specials chalkboard, deliberating ordering wine and causing a record scratch scene. That's when I saw the sign:

Shot & a Beer $11

Beer: **BUD**

Dad, your name is all over bars, and you would love this one. Elizabeth straightened up, grabbed the bar with both hands, and raised her voice just enough to order a pinot noir, but I was no longer there. Instead, I was my 10-year-old self, turning circles on the stool next to you, as you strummed your fingers on the bar.

Through the years, our quality time moved from Sunday morning dippy eggs (known as sunny-side up outside of good 'ol Pennsylvania) at Margaret's Diner to late afternoons "tying one on" at the Eagle Tavern or Lasorda's or Ron's. Those restaurants where you'd repeat that old line: "Food stinks, but the portions are huge." Errands and pick-ups were your cover story. A pick-up from my friend's house included a drinking detour, and I gladly played your cover.

Quick: What's the greatest cover of all time? I'd say Joe Cocker's "With a Little Help from My Friends." Arguably better than the original, and to beat The Beatles? Impressive.

> **No, the greatest cover of all time is Tina doing John Fogerty's "Proud Mary." "*We never ever do nothing nice and easy. We always do it nice and rough.*" If you're gonna bust my balls about drinking, then this is gonna be nice and rough.**

Well, *with a little help from your daughter*, your cover was set. Looking back, I see how screwed up our quality time was together, and yet I wouldn't trade it for anything except a winning Powerball ticket. Bars are a fun place for kids from about the ages of 8 to 15. Too young and you can't sit still, too old and you want a real drink. I frequented taverns with you from my bowl cut to my perm. My drink of choice: a Shirley Temple, *two* cherries. I observed that drink ordering was specific: neat, rocks, up, twist, olive, onion, shake, or stir. So, I doubled down on the cherries. Bartenders considered me a novelty, giving me pretzels or peanuts if they had them. If not, then a pile of orange slices. Waitresses would come by to say hello because at two in the afternoon, tables are empty.

Smelling that coastside bar's stale beer mixed with 20-year-old cigarette smoke that won't dissipate from its wooden paneled walls, my scalp tingled as I felt you there. Is this what people feel when they visit a gravesite?

As Elizabeth and I took our afternoon drinks to a table, I reflexively looked back at the bar, searching for your rotund head angled up at the TV because you'd bet the spread. How long were our cover-up outings in bars like this? My memory has distorted them.

I do remember that ounce for ounce, it takes a kid a lot less time to drink a Shirley Temple, pretend to watch ESPN, and answer "What's your name? How old are you? Isn't your dad funny?" than it takes to enjoy a scotch or two.

I always ended up bored, but I still wanted to be in the club. If time permitted, we'd order food: A BLT for you, chicken fingers and fries for me. Or was lunch part of the cover? "We grabbed a bite," you'd say as we walked in the door, fooling no one but me. I don't know much of anything about parenting, but I'm pretty sure the phrase "Don't tell your mother" should be reserved for a Mother's Day gift.

"This one doesn't tell the wife," or "She doesn't rat me out like her sister does," you'd confide in whoever sat next to us. And they would laugh, and I would laugh into my straw, making bubbles, not getting the joke. I was part of the gang—without any clue what our crime was.

Your drinking was not the stuff they make movies about. It's not even the stuff they write books about. It was functional and common. There's an f-bomb to throw your way, a buck for the swear jar: You were a **F**unctional Alcoholic. It was death by a thousand nips.

What I learned in the gang is if you're gonna have only a few, make 'em the strong stuff. Start with a scotch, or better yet, two vodka martinis (packs the same punch and leaves no smell). If smell isn't an issue, end with Budweiser.

As I got older, you would lecture me to pick one drink and drink it all night. "Never mix your liquors, or you'll get sick. But you can always end with a beer." And with this routine, it's easiest to run a tab.

I was shamefully old when I learned that carrying tabs at restaurants wasn't part of adulthood, like taxes or electric bills. I also realized that I had a larger vocabulary for drinking than my friends did. They never used phrases like "having a couple pops," "a nip," "grabbing a Bud," "tying one on," "ending up half in the bag," "shitfaced," "potted," "bombed," or "in the cups." Is this generational language, or did our house require more words for the activity?

My brain is still twisted up with memories of our drinking days, and after all the lies and the tension you caused, after watching the drink slowly kill you, I sat in that harbor bar sipping on their house wine, pretending to watch the 49ers, thinking how cool I'd be if I ran a tab there.

Somewhere in my twenties, around the time I learned tavern tabs weren't a recurring household expense, I could finally recognize if you were bombed. When you were half in the bag, you had an anger about you. Your eyes would be glassy and laser-focused at the same time, looking to clash. Also in my twenties, Robyn had to tell me you were an alcoholic, what a proverbial drink in the face. Before that, I thought *Dad has a tough job,* and *Kids aren't supposed to ask for the remote ever.*

In addition to explaining that you were an alcoholic, Robyn had to tell me, "And it's gonna kill him."

"Nothing will kill that bastard," I probably joked.

"He's got a heart condition; he can't drink like this." She set me straight. A few pops every day for 35 years; add in a bad heart and some weak lungs, and that should do it.

I didn't *really* drink until well into my thirties. I went to college, started smoking, got a teaching job, met your mother, bought a house, quit smoking on November 21, 1974, when the first kid arrived, got a better job, and bought another house, all without booze. Took a bigger job, first superintendency. The school board, my new boss, liked to tie one on. New job, new town, fitting in with new people. It began nice and easy, that gene slowly kicking in somewhere around 34.

You were also 34 when I was born and kept a glass in your hand all the time. When I was really little and couldn't yet reach a counter, around the time when our ritual was for you to give me the first sip of your beer, Mom told me you had *extra heart*. She meant it in every sense, but particularly that the wall in your heart was thicker than usual, making it harder to pump blood. Add in alcohol, and so began your periodic hospital visits to get "zapped" out of AFib.

I don't know what your drinking was like for her. What was harder: the drinking itself, or your denial of the slow death it was causing? After you died, your doctor tried to impress upon Mom that everything she did, the healthy cooking, the constant researching for (your word: tasteless) low salt alternatives, the nudging you to make and then go to doctor appointments, had added years onto you. These days, Mom's energy goes to watching us each time a drink touches our lips, waiting to see if the gene will kick in.

When you retired for a year, without employment to curb your thirst, that was your *least* functional time, bottom of the glass, so to speak. We had recently gotten Sophie the Dog, and you'd sit on the back porch, talking about life to a puppy. Probably saying: "I wanna to move to a town that ends in 'burg,' where there's nothing going. Everyone would call me Doc."

But I was away at college, and when I came home, laundry in hand and a bit hungover myself, Mom and Robyn had created their own club: going to Al-Anon. You weren't in AA, but there they were in Al-Anon meetings. You must have known where they were going because who gets up after weekday dinner in the suburbs and goes *anywhere*?

One time, home for the summer, I accidentally cornered you when I innocently asked where Mom was. You had to respond, "She went to her meeting." You didn't move your eyes from the TV. I was too young to know that shame can look like rage. I nodded and slunk out of the room. Like your drinking, Al-Anon became a truth almost never spoken aloud.

I agreed with Mom and Robyn that you were an alcoholic, and I still went to "lunches" with you, never snitching. I wanted to be everyone's favorite. I went to two whole Al-Anon meetings. I dragged an extra folding chair across the church basement floor, making that patented screech of metal on tile, to join the circle next to Mom and Robyn.

A mother, sitting next to her husband, described their adult son's drug addiction. It was something hard involving needles. They had kicked him out of the house, but recently let him back in sober. My throat stuck. *What in the hell are we doing in this hell?*

Mom and Robyn both shared, describing your drinking and how it made you an absolute dick (I'm quoting verbatim there). But when they said, "and he's gonna die," that was the killer (pun intended). When they were done and it was my turn by order of circle law, I pointed to them, shook my head, asking to be skipped, and managed an "I'm with them." Were we trying to save you or ourselves? I wasn't sure. But damn if I didn't pick right up on the Al-Anon teachings: *Live your own life because you can't control the life of your addict.* Maybe that's why you said "No forced marches" all the time.

It was around this time, drunk on strawberry Boone's "wine," when I finally said to a friend, almost inaudible, trying it out: "My dad's an alcoholic." To my shock, the friend countered: "My mom's an alcoholic." Well, that sure as shit made no sense. *Dads* drank. Moms packed your lunch and wrote notes on your napkins:

> *Jenny LaBoopee:*
> *Winner, Winner*
> *Chicken Dinner!*
> *No really, that's what we're having for dinner tonight.*
> *Love, –M*

What did an alcoholic mom even look like? How could a drunk mom change sheets, press jeans, fold underwear, grow science project crystals, and string up a solar system out of embroidery hoops and Styrofoam balls? When I asked *you* for help with school, you delivered your classic line: "I already did (insert grade). Now it's your turn."

That college friend—we've stayed in touch all these years, always with a wink of understanding, but I'm not sure I do. The story of the functional alcoholic isn't exceptional, except that it looks a bit different in every house. For the functional alcoholic, the bottle shaves off years, and there's rarely a way to prove it. Seems these alcoholics always get credit for dying from something else, something beyond their control and unfortunate, like massive heart failure. Only their family knows, and we don't get to blame them for leaving years on the table. But if we had to bet on your life, we would still have taken the under.

Look, drinking is relative—*all my* relatives. I don't know if you've got the gene. I had that gene coming in from all sides: the Irish and the Polish. I tried an AA meeting, but I couldn't stomach all the God. People change, just not the way you want them to, I—

—Wait, that's not what you would say. Even now, I don't think you'd say much of anything. You'd probably use it as a chance to repeat a good line.

Like that time we were all sitting around the TV—that same TV that your mother *watered*. Nowadays, TVs are paper-thin and hang on walls. This was one of those big '90s boxes, deeper than my Dodge Intrepid was wide. She placed a damn plant on top for "decoration," and then watered it, which, if you understand how wicker baskets work, also watered my TV. After that, we had to smack it on the side for the sound to come on, but smacking it worked.

So, we were all around that water TV. I was on my couch. You kids were lying on the floor, eyeballs as close as possible. Your mother was ironing. She could never sit still and watch a show. Always doing something.

One of those anti-drug commercials came on, something about "This is your brain on drugs," showing an egg frying in a pan. As the commercial ended, I took the parenting opportunity and muted the often self-muted TV.

"Kids, listen up," I started in with my school-board-meeting voice. Your mother even looked up, stopping the back and forth of the iron. "If you're ever at a party and there's drinking. Either you're drinking or your ride is drinking; you call me. I don't care what time it is. Middle of the night, you call me."

Your mother's eyes fixed on me in admiration.

So, I finished my thought: "And if I'm sober, I'll come pick you up."

Your mother slammed down the iron and walked out. Imagine that, walking out on one of my best lines. Sometimes my straight man was just too straight.

That sounds like you. Now, back at the beach bar, I moseyed back up to the bar, stared at the **Bud** signs, and ordered another round of house red for Elizabeth and me. Felt good to be out of the house at "lunch."

10

"My heart going 'Boom-boom-boom.'
'Hey,' I said
'You can keep my things,
They've come to take me home.'"

—Peter Gabriel

This summer, Robyn bought the house—*your* house.

Your sister never would cut the umbilical cord, and you moved across the damn country. Somewhere between you two is a normal kid (probably your brother).

Mom booked the movers for July 23rd, moving out of your house on the third anniversary of your death. I immediately called Robyn to talk-yell, as only sisters can, about the *exact* day you died. Robyn insisted I was wrong, that you passed on the 24th or the 25th, and that Mom was *not* moving on your death date. I tried recalling the order of events (was it a Tuesday I got the call?), not so much because it mattered, but because I love winning.

> *Housewarming gift idea: A tasteful needlepoint that says: "A Sister Is a Friend You Don't Have to Be Nice To."*

The death certificate claims July 24th: can't argue with that, except that we do. I remember when the certificate was delivered, Mom, rubbing her thumbnail against her upper lip, commented that it wasn't the right date, and in that state of griever exhaustion, resigned to the mistake. "Great, now we have two days of hell to get through each year instead of one." The debate continued, with Robyn and me once again pointing fingers at the funeral home as the culprit, as if it matters. And it matters because when you are going through hell, it's important to find someone to blame.

The funeral director's email included a quote under her signature along the lines of: "*A smile is like an upside-down rainbow. It sends out little splashes of joy even after the darkest storms.*"

Fuck you, Deborah.

> *Why do they call it a funeral "home"? Nothing homey in that place. At least a "parlor" is where they turn tricks, and this racket felt like a lot of tricks.*

The business of death requires throwing money at rushed decisions as if making the expensive, quick choices will bring the person back. The tricks were most obvious when they made us sign a government-issued disclosure, attesting that they weren't taking advantage of us in our time of need. I signed on the line, but stole their pen.

The way Nani Lil did it, planning her entire funeral down to the readings, the flowers, what she would wear (do people see shoes in a casket?), is the way to go if you care. You didn't care, but that left us without instructions, making wrong decisions, and throwing your money around.

When Mom and I were traveling back from Luxembourg to get to you, it was Bryan-Ever-the-Big-Brother making all the decisions. First, the coroner said they wouldn't keep your body, and we needed a funeral home or somewhere for it to go *immediately*. Enter the funeral home, asking if we wanted to have your body embalmed. Not even sure what all that meant, we said yes. Since you ended up being cremated, that was $4,500 up in smoke.

Then they asked about a viewing, which Mom knew you did not want, but the devout Catholics in the family (all four of them) did. Mom asked them to remove all 100 chairs so that it wasn't a "viewing." Deborah refused, claiming she had nowhere to put them. In the end, they charged us $1,000 to put you in a room of empty seats. It looked like a concert venue once the roadies took the stage to pack up and tear down.

Mom and I sat motionless, numb in the director's office that faced a highway and smelled like curtain dust. We spent a week there that afternoon. Like Harry Chapin's favorite song, we knew that "… anywhere's a better place to be." Robyn stayed home, honoring your wishes and pointing out how proud you'd be that tickets to see you cost $250.

I'm glad your mom stuck by me with no funeral. Those Catholics in the family, at the university, and even my friends—especially the priest (God save him), I bet they all gave Jeannie a ton of shit for not having a funeral. I never believed in water on the baby, the god-awful God music, and a man who's never been married running Pre-Cana classes for couples as if he knows how to love someone after 40 years of bad breath and gas. You have to fart in front of your spouse right away, or else it's going to be a long life. Priests don't get that.

And if you were a Catholic when I was a Catholic, then you'd *really* know why no funeral for me. I'm talking Catholic school in the '50s and '60s. For starters, those nuns beat the shit out of us. You ever see the nun scene in the movie *Blues Brothers*? She takes a yardstick and beats the crap out of Dan Aykroyd and

John Belushi. Then, when the first stick breaks, she gets an even *bigger* stick. That's not fiction. That's a goddamn documentary. My "filthy mouth" and "bad attitude" went to Monsignor Bonner Catholic High School and barely survived. Even on the good days, when I happened to answer a question right and was invited to move up to the front of the class (an honor), the nun made it clear: "Leave your books, Stefanski. You'll be back there."

And in case you think the media, the movies, and the lawsuits have it wrong—they don't. In my seventh-grade gym class at an all-boys Catholic school, we ran the mile naked for "health" reasons. Give me a fucking break. No funeral. Not giving them any more of my time or money. Lucky for you, I left no money, just the kind of debt that died with me.

And then, they botched up your "urn." I had only brought them one 22 oz. Melitta coffee can from my Acme errand, assuming one large can was enough. It wasn't. On the day they delivered you to the house, they brought half of you in the coffee can and the other half of you in a white cardboard box, bigger than chocolates, smaller than shoe.

They never called to tell me you didn't fit and to bring another can. Probably, Deborah thought the coffee can was a joke. And it was. It was a joke on funerals and funeral homes, on religion and on rituals, and it was your own sermon on what really defines a life. Mom and I dumped the rest of you in the second coffee can ourselves. We didn't charge you a dime.

The last time I enjoyed anything close to a religious ritual was back in the '80s in that Western Pennsylvania town we lived in, built up around a brickyard used for the steel industry. Back when you were too little to go to Sunday school with your brother and sister. At that time, God knows why, your mother was *teaching* Sunday school. This left you and me fending for ourselves on the Lord's Day.

You were what, three or four? We'd go to Peggy's Diner, that one-story brick building off Rte. 220, with its fiberglass ceiling and diagonal wood paneled walls. It smelled of burnt coffee and fried food, and they didn't even charge you extra for that salty smell that stuck to your clothes when you left. And since we were so highbrow, we never, ever called it Peggy's. To us, it was Margaret's.

They sold toys behind the counter, and staring at that garbage kept you occupied. We never looked at a menu. You couldn't read, and no one should need a breakfast menu at a diner. You always ordered eggy and toast. I got the scrapple and bought a lotto ticket, still no regrets there. Now Margaret's, with its regulars, its *"How ya been?"* That's ritual, and that's a religion I can get behind.

Everybody knew everybody in that burg. Doc was the town doctor; his son Denny was the dentist. Doc's wife, Maxine, was in the business of everybody's business. And everyone and their son was named Richard, Rich, Rick, or Dicky. When we first moved into our split-level with the gravel driveway, your mother was calling around to invite some school board members to dinner when an unidentified male answered the phone:

"Oh, hello. I'm sorry. Is this Big Dicky or Little Dicky?" she innocently asked, getting her bearings.

"Lady, I don't think I know you well enough yet to answer that." Damn, I miss that place.

We ended up leaving our split-level, Margaret's, and that "burg" in Western PA. We had culture shock when we first got there, calling it Hicksville, Podunk, The Boonies, The Sticks. And it's true that growing up there, at the ripe age of 11, your brother asked us what a museum was and why I didn't hunt like the other dads. But it was in The Sticks where we found some of the best people we'd ever meet. They were the people you want at your funeral—if you have one.

We moved in '86 to the house you would call home, now your sister's. That was back when people got so much more for their money out there, although it was a solid hour from Philly and my new job. The town was a bit of a cow field, but the school test scores were decent. Being from Philadelphia, this move felt like going home except with deer ticks, but still, like Western PA, lacking any real diversity.

Thirty-five years in that house. Turns out, Robyn buying the house, your house, was the only way it could go down. Three years after your death and the weight of that house was crippling Mom's tiny frame. Like "Hotel California," Mom needed to check out, but she could never leave.

Even before any talk of moving, every time I went home to visit, I tried to get Mom to throw things out, so we could breathe. I'd find a potentially tossable book, a biography of a baseball player, or a politician.

"His brother gave him that!" she'd say, in shock that I would throw out such a family heirloom.

"But did he ever *read* it?" I'd ask. She'd answer, "No," while placing the book back on the shelf under the coffee table. Mom's not a hoarder, but with a little more practice, I think she could get there.

I know. When we redid that kitchen, she made me put cabinets everywhere, fill every inch with shit. Before that, the refrigerator stood alone. And when you were little, right when I got home from work, before the tie came off, I would pick you up and sit you on the top of the fridge. You loved that crap. You'd sit up there for hours if I let you. You were such a mouthy kid; I was trying to get you to shut up for a few minutes. I never got to put my grandkids up there because of those cabinets and my own kid's overprotective parenting.

I wonder how jam-packed that basement was. Did they find my shoe-shining kits, dried-up jars of polish from my working days?

I used to let you smell the tins, a little legal high like markers or gasoline.

Moving was a feat. Or at least it looked like it. Of course, I wasn't there to help. I was across the country, judging and trying to control from afar. I had absolutely no hope that it would all be done in time for these moving men scheduled so unceremoniously on July 23rd. The equation looked like this:

Mom

(Grieving widow, budding hoarder, with a new chiweenie rescue dog likely to run away through any door crack opening, trying to pack up a house chock full of 35 years of stuff, which included gold-painted macaroni art from the '80s.)

+

Robyn

(Single mom of four—including apathetic teenage boys, battling untreated and self-diagnosed attention deficit disorder, moving out of a rental unit utterly destroyed by her brood, plus a pandemic puppy she picked up, to merge households with her partner—also a single parent of two girls.)

= Einstein's Theory of Chaos

(Six kids in your house.)

But let me tell you, these two are deterministic chaos. I'd never say it to their faces, but there's nothing their zig-zagged brains can't do. You're missing it, but as time goes on, they're getting more and more alike. Their Italian noses and high cheekbones are starting to match. They seem to be the only ones to follow each other's stories, weaving from middle to end to start.

During the weeks leading up to the move, I got a call from Robyn.

"So, Mom and I decided to clean out the attic today." I can barely make out her voice through snort-laughing. "Right off the bat, Mom is lecturing me." She softens her voice and raises it a couple of octaves for her Mom-pression: "Now there's a lot of stuff up here. I've got stuff from your childhood and even my grandmother's things. You have to go slow, and let me look through it. I won't be pushed into getting rid of it."

They pulled on the frayed cord hanging from the garage ceiling, bringing the attic door and its collapsible ladder creaking down from above. It's still cracked down the left side where it was (shoddily) patched together with an extra piece of wood. Still gives out by several inches whenever pressure is put on it. Was that fix your chubby handiwork?

Mighta been. I never did any of the things I talked about, like putting a pool in the backyard, a hot tub in the sunroom, or finishing the basement. But man, I loved that house. It was a *good* house. Cramped in all the right places.

I remember the summer of '87 when we first pulled our Pontiac into the driveway. Even back then, the red aluminum siding was fading. To my 40-year-old eyes, that four-bedroom, two-and-a-half bath sitting on a whole acre of land was a goddamn mansion.

As the musty attic smell hit them, all 100 lbs. of Mom climbed the wobbly ladder, still lecturing Robyn. "*I mean it. Don't pressure me. These are important memor—*"

Half-submerged in the attic, giving her a full view of the room, she stopped mid-sentence and turned to Robyn. "It's empty."

Your craftsman ladder shakes with Robyn's laughter. The accusations start as Mom struggles to make it down safely. "Where is my stuff? I bet Jenny threw it out last time she was here."

Robyn could barely stop squawking her impressions of Mom into the phone long enough to ask if this was my doing: *"This is very important stuff, and you need to respect these things."*

"Put Mom on the phone," I instruct. "Mom, you don't remember? Back in May, we cleaned out the attic, filled the car, and took all that crap over to Uncle Bob's. He had rented one of those dumpsters."

"But what was up there?"

"I dunno, old Halloween costumes, some handmade doilies from your grandmother, and a lot of mouse shit. We kept the mouse shit."

"My attic is empty. In every sense of the phrase." She's resigned.

In the end, they didn't move everything. Their agreement was that Mom could take anything she wanted and leave whatever she didn't, and then all that crapola would become Robyn's problem.

Moving is hard, and things get left behind. Some things they agreed they'd move later, like holiday decorations not needed for months, or ever, one could argue.

Other arguably more important possessions, *almost* got lost in the shuffle—including you.

Wondering where you've been spending your days? Don't forget, you had to be placed in not one, but *two large* cans. One of the tins we took to your golf course and spread out along your favorite hole, another situation I did not ask enough questions about. Did the country club approve this? Two of your golf buddies—Bill and Bill—met us there in the parking lot with carts to take us to your favorite hole. It was winter in southeastern Pennsylvania, so there were no golfers asking to play through as we sprinkled you around the green.

I do recall that there was a lot more of *you* than when I've seen this done in the movies. There, loved ones are standing on a bridge positioned over a fast-moving river or on a boat with the sun setting over a warm day, while the ocean plays its soothing soundtrack. Everyone takes a handful and, dramatically, spiritually, and uniformly, sprinkles the ashes of their deceased into the flowing water. There are so many critical stages, lighting, and sound choices in that setting that we failed to replicate.

Instead, we gathered in the dead of winter over frozen turf. We each needed to take *many* gloves full. This was not a one-and-done situation. Your dust did not fly in any wind. No sir, your dust dropped on our shoes. I said a few words before we started, never looking up from the paper I typed them on, probably just about how you would hate this display of affection. Otherwise, there was no river or ocean to drown out the silence.

The task felt never-ending. Thank God, Mom only brought one of your cans. And we couldn't just flip the can over and leave you all piled up on the 13th hole. It's called *"spreading* the ashes." Would we have dumped most of you behind a bush if your golfing buddies hadn't joined us? Probably.

Regardless of whether the river or ocean holds any actual meaning to the deceased, I now know people pick bodies of water because ashes can poetically float away; spirituality is baked right in. It's hard for me to feign faith at a golf course, even if that was your Heaven.

This left another can of you at home. Mom kept you in a dresser drawer in the bedroom. Not *your* dresser, just *a* dresser. Once, when I'd come home to visit, I pulled you out to screw with Robyn. "Hey, can you come in here?" I lured her into her old bedroom where I had your can on the pillow next to me, pretending to read to you from one of the books Mom bought that you never read, this one titled *How Not to Die: Discover the Foods Scientifically Proven to Prevent and Reverse Disease.*

The day before the movers were set to come, Robyn was at your house, helping to make sure Mom was packed and ready. She went into that same bedroom for a final check, as Mom yelled from across the hall, "Don't open that! Dad's in there!"

Robyn continued opening dresser drawers. There you were, all 22 ounces of you, left behind.

So, your mother left me behind in the house? I don't mind. George Thorogood put it best: "… *that don't befront me.*" Good job with the ashes you did get rid of. Plus, I didn't leave much in the way of instructions. Most importantly, I really don't care.

But what *did* Mom remember to pack? Your dirty laundry. Your hamper has never been emptied. This is literal "dirty laundry" we are not permitted to air outside of the family. I'm not going to pretend I didn't give it a sniff every now and then. But after about a year, it lost your salty smell of Budweiser, pretzels, and the sweat that comes with a bad heart. Your hamper was picked up and moved in its entirety to the new house. But you, yourself, were forgotten. Luckily, we know the new buyers.

You should know that after all this, I don't have many regrets.

I went to a shitty movie once with my buddies and said, "Let's leave." But they insisted, "We already paid for the tickets." It's a short ride. Leave the shitty movies.

Maybe a last regret from the late '80s, too. Roy Orbison was touring with Jerry Lee Lewis. Jeannie and I were going to get tickets, but changed our minds. "I'll see him next time around," I said. Then that fucker up and died on me. Died the same way I did. Heart attack at 52 at his mother's house.

And did you know "(Baby) You've Got What It Takes" was released *after* he died? Written by Petty, too. Roy was posthumously nominated for a Grammy. People can still do shit when they're dead, but best to do it in life. So, go to the concert. Take the trip.

Take your *mother* on the trip—make her travel again. And make her throw out my laundry.

Well, your house felt dead, your Olympic-level snoring no longer reverberating through the paper-thin walls. But now it's full again. Six kids. Couches everywhere while they merge two houses into one. New puppy eating shoes. Construction workers finally finished that basement. High-school-kid clunker cars line the street in front, blocking the neighbor's driveway. The house breathes life again, but also smells like the piss and pits of teenage boys.

The Encore

"The mother and child reunion is only a motion away."
—Paul Simon

Mom plops herself down to wait on the marble bench, leaning her head against the marble wall as her wheely luggage gently glides on its own down the ancient, tilted floor, also marble. Marble: Greece's linoleum? I pace the lobby, a foyer of a once-mansion. I insisted on booking a boutique hotel in Athens, where the friendly but casual staff are rarely at their makeshift desk in this "lobby."

Where is our driver? I'm a stickler for the 3-Hours-Before-When-Traveling-Internationally Rule that another left-brained Virgo likely made up. Congratulating myself on using some Greek taxi app the internet recommended, I call the driver.

"I am here," he spits.

I lean my top half out the front doors, scanning up and down the narrow side street of this hotel-house. I don't see any cars. Boutique can mean hidden, so I add "Monsieur Didot, yes?"

"FUCK!" he Greek-yells the universal English word that breaks down cultural boundaries. "I am wrong hotel. Ten minutes."

On a 20-minute drive to the airport, the Acropolis keeps eyes on us from above as we take our last glimpse of Greece. I'm still in disbelief that Mom traveled again. Was she all talk, saying she would never leave the country again after we left Luxembourg to get home to you? Was it the pandemic lockdown these last few years that made her stir crazy enough? Was it the lure of a destination yoga retreat? Wellness vacations are all the rage. Or was it the DNA test I took that told us we are as much Greek as we are Italian?

> *Learning family ancestry through DNA is as popular as wellness vacations these days.*

People are finding out that their traveling salesman father had another family, they thought they were 100% Chinese, and they are, or that their true family origin is about 30 marathon lengths down and to the right.

Finding out that my Italian ass is actually Greek better explains my nose. I tried telling Nani Lil when she was still here, but she would have none of it. Italian always and forever, all ~~100~~ 99 years.

Whatever got us here, Mom is back. Hiking Santorini's famous 7-mile trail from Oia to Fira, popping her head in each and every unlocked church door, doing a yogi handstand up the wall, and downing her entire shot of complimentary ouzo. Don't sniff, shoot. I threw mine over the side of the boat we were on. She got her spirit back in what we now know is our homeland.

Still with plenty of time, the driver places all our bags on the curb and rejoins the traffic crawl from the airport. We pause at a wall of departure screens to find our counter. I've never seen counter numbers in the three digits as the rows of airline brands stretch on and on. After circling for a bit, we find our counter, and Mom maneuvers her bag onto the scale.

"Your passport and boarding pass, please," says the attendant.

Mom looks at me. "I don't have it," her lips barely moving.

"Which one?"

"Either. I don't have my purse," she comments, as if this was the plan all along.

"Is it at the hotel or in the cab?" I'm confused by her calmness.

"I don't know." She remains motionless, another Greek statue.

I begin calling the hotel, picturing the empty desk in the foyer as the rings pile up.

I call our driver through the taxi app. One look in the rearview mirror, and he locates the purse. We wheel ourselves back out to the curb for the interception and smile, call to, wave at, and make asses of ourselves for every black van that passes. In the time it took us to get rejected by the counter lady, the driver made it pretty far.

Finally, the right black van screeches to a stop in front of us. "Thank you!" Mom starts hugging the driver, reaching into her forgotten purse and taking out the American dollars she has left. "This is all I have. Can you use this?" Her hands are now around his face. I'm scared she may kiss him. Or maybe our people do that here? He nods and wiggles free, jumping back into the traffic. We retrace our steps to the counter.

"How were you so calm?" I ask.

"I might have been in shock? But now that it worked out, I'll pretend I'm wise. Your grandmother used to say: 'There are worse things than death.' I'll paraphrase her and say: There are worse things than losing your passport."

I'm already booking our next yoga retreat. We'll head to the town in Italy where Mom's grandparents were born. Apparently, our Greek is *quite a few* generations back. She's located a cousin in his nineties for us to drop in on—if he doesn't drop first. I'll carry the passports.

Afterword on the Afterlife

Remembering those we've lost with a little laughter, without pain, even temporarily, is a gift. In *A Light Roast*, Jen Stefanski writes conversations with her deceased father. With great writing, it's as if the departed have visited us as vividly as in a dream. Whom do you dream of?

I dream of my beloved pets. Or my mother. My father, too. My sister, my grandmother. And I embrace them.

Sometimes, they speak to me or hand me a bite to eat. Or ask me to get in, driving me across a bridge on misted waters. I take their offers, though it's taboo, I've been told, to accept anything from the dead, even if it's only a dream.

They're as three-dimensional as they were in life. I don't discern the difference until I wake, when I remember that they're gone, but it feels as though we've visited. I can still feel the warm purr of my childhood cat burrowing her nose in my armpit. Or smell the soup as I enter my mother's apartment, my shoes clacking on her parquet floor. Or hear my father's haughty voice, calling me by my name.

When I initially read Jen Stefanski's early chapters of *A Light Roast* through an online writer's group, of course, I welcomed Bud. I laughed out loud at Jen's distinct humor, at her Nani motioning to her crotch with her hands full of eggy breadcrumbs, and her father Bud teaching her "how to get four uses out of the same pair of underwear."

Bud's narrative is depicted with such clarity that I could almost hear him proclaim that "Life is a shit sandwich." His colorful, expressive character reminds me of my own departed loved ones, the kind they don't make anymore. But I still dream.

Who is it that visits you?

–Tara Lee O'Brien

Author of *Jackpot Junkie: A Memoir on Luck*

Acknowledgments

With a little help from my friends...

Shit, we did it! And by "we," I mean all of the people who helped bring Bud back into the world. Without the encouragement and support of these fine folks, this would still be an idea and maybe a journal entry. These people taught me that anything is possible, everyone is A Creative, and that Bud is still here.

Thank you, Linsey Krolik, the first person who gave me confidence when I whispered to her over wine: *"I wish I were a writer, because I have an idea."* She only ever assumed this was possible. Linsey, I love how you see this world! And thanks to Regina Colantonio, a wonder woman who believes down to her bones that we can do anything, and whose passion is contagious. Thank you, Vicky Regan, Tyndie DuBose, Lori Schak, & Kelly McQuage, for your encouragement and genuine desire to read drafts. Thanks to Adrienne Go for your motivation as a fellow lawyer-turned-author.

I'm grateful for the writing courses at Stanford's Continuing Studies program and their talented instructors. Thank you, Rebecca Schuman, Lynn Stegner, Anne Zimmerman, and Rachel Smith, who patiently shared their skills and provided invaluable feedback. In my first memoir class, I met four authors willing to start a writing group. So big, huge thanks to Donna Zuckerberg, Beth Gilson, Caroline van de Pol, and Tara Lee O'Brien, who gave me their time and guidance and the ability to just keep going. You all read a shitty first draft and just-as-shitty second drafts with patience, kindness, and great insight. Extra thanks to Caroline and Tara, who read to the end, believing in the reality of these conversations. Thank you, Caroline, for constant book therapy. Thank you, Tara, for telling me I was finished and to just put it out there. And for giving me some of the best advice I've ever received: *"Fuck 'em."* Applicable in so many of life's situations …

Thank you to the other female authors I'll never meet but whose written-down wisdom I turned to again and again: Julia Cameron's *The Artist's Way*; Anne Lamont's *Bird by Bird*; and Elizabeth Gilbert's *Big Magic*. These works give us all permission to be Creatives, no matter how the world has tried to define us.

Thank you, Hilary Jastram and Bookmark Publishing. You somehow understood this labor of love from the get-go. I didn't believe you when you said finishing and publishing a book should be fun. And yet, somehow, you made it so. Thank you for your expertise, hard work, and caring for this project and Bud.

Thank you to my lifelong friend and now cover designer, Karen Nickerson, for acting like it was totally normal that I wrote a book. Your expert talent and vision are what brought this all to life. Cheers to you! You've got Cliff's encyclopedia of knowledge with the loyalty of Norm—thanks for your friendship and always saving me a barstool.

Thank you, Rusty, my biggest critic and biggest fan—cause that's marriage, right? I couldn't have done this without your support and encouragement, and the way you heard Bud's voice immediately. Above all, thank you for going through this life with me. I love you madly.

Thank you, Bryan, my big brother, no matter how old I get. You never asked for the gig, but you do it so well.

Thank you to my sister, Robyn, for building me up and knocking me down—as only a sister can, and always right when I need it. Thank you for cutting your heart open again to read this book and write the foreword. You are the true Creative, and I am excited to watch the "back nine" of your life ('cause you're *so much* older than me).

Thank you to my mom for letting me do this and for being my fact-checker. Thank you for showing me how to go through life with creativity and imagination. You are funnier than you realize, but I would never tell you that to your face—it ain't our style.

And, of course, thanks to Bud, who would absolutely despise being in a book. Thank you for the stories, and thank you for the music. Please join me in sending Bud off with a song:

🎶 *Here's to you, Bud Stefanski, here's to you.*

Here's to you, Bud Stefanski, here's to you.

Oh, you think you're upper class,

But you're just a horse's ass.

Here's to you, Bud Stefanski, here's to you. 🎶

Everything I need to know in life I learned from my old man with his big, bad heart.

- You "lay" something down; people "lie" down.
- The Eagles' "Take It Easy" was written by Jackson Browne.
- If you're in a situation where you can't curse, make up a word: I suggest crunt.
- Seger helped the Eagles write "Heartache Tonight." They needed a chorus, and Glenn called up his buddy.
- Never lease a car.
- The spouse who does the finances gets to skim off the top.
- There are five guitar solos in Rod "The Bod" Stewart's "Maggie May," 'cause if something's good, keep doing it.
- Almost no one can spell diarrhea—go ahead, ask around.
- Wear thick socks—heat comes out of your feet.
- *Really listen* to the lyrics, or you'll end up like Reagan playing "Born in the U.S.A." at his campaign rallies.
  - The lyrics to Fogerty's "Centerfield" are "Put me in, *Coach,*" not "Put me in *cold.*"
  - But the lyrics to Skynyrd's "Free Bird" are "And this bird you cannot change," when we all know it should be "and this bird you cannot *cage.*"
- Get your spouse flowers, but only *give* them in front of other people, then you look really good.
- The only good Jesus song is "Spirit in the Sky," and Greenbaum was Jewish—go figure.
- Sometimes it just feels good to cry.
- No forced marches.
- Keep your debt till you die, and it dies with you.
- If the world were perfect, it wouldn't be. Now that gem's from Yogi Berra.

About the Authors

Dr. Charles F. Stefanski is the author of a doctoral dissertation, but the title is too long to include here. In 1965, he published a controversial opinion piece in St. Joe's University student newspaper, *The Hawk*, arguing that the cafeteria food was really not that bad. He was an English teacher, a school administrator, and a professor. As a toddler, he was nicknamed "My Buddy" by his older brother, Bob, and thereafter went by Bud. Bud currently resides in a Melitta coffee can located in a dresser drawer in Honey Brook, Pennsylvania, and somewhere on the 13th hole of Schuylkill Country Club. He promised his wife he would leave his offbeat brain to science, but we forgot and cremated all of him. So, his wit and wisdom are in this book instead.

Jennifer Stefanski is Bud's daughter and the author of a 1999 essay published in *Scholastic News Magazine* (thanks, Mr. Stewart!), describing the renowned 20th-century inventor and plumber, Thomas Crapper, and his impact on her favorite invention: The Toilet. In her day job as a lawyer, she authors numerous website disclosures that she's worried you've failed to read. This is her debut book. She lives in Half Moon Bay, California, with her husband, Rusty, and their dog, Stevie Licks.

www.ingramcontent.com/pod-product-compliance
Lightning Source LLC
Chambersburg PA
CBHW060432130626
46555CB00005B/2327